Freshwater Theatre Press

# Better (or) Worse

Freshwater Theatre

Freshwater Theatre Press

Copyright © 2012 Freshwater Press

Freshwater Theatre Press

## DEDICATION

The state legislature asked us to define marriage.  We decided to give it a shot.

This show was originally produced as a fundraiser for Minnesotans United for All Marriage, as part of the effort to defeat the amendment to alter our state's constitution to limit the definition of marriage to "one man, one woman."

To the beautiful and talented artists who donated their time and craft to bring this show to the stage, thank you with all of our hearts.

And to Minnesota.

We did it.

*Love, Freshwater Theatre*

Freshwater Theatre Press

Freshwater Theatre Press

Freshwater Theatre Press

# CONTENTS

| | | |
|---|---|---|
| | Information on Royalties | i |
| 1 | Ebbing | 5 |
| 2 | Second Wedding | 20 |
| 3 | HomeWrecker | 25 |
| 4 | Do You Think This Looks Gay on Me? | 27 |
| 5 | Pelican Girls | 37 |
| 6 | Schadenfreude | 40 |
| 7 | I could never live in a Social Democracy. The lines are too long. | 60 |
| 8 | Poplin | 67 |
| 9 | Since the Kids are Gone | 77 |
| 10 | Scars | 90 |
| 11 | Waiting | 103 |
| 12 | A Small Play about Marriage | 108 |
| 13 | The Entr'actes | 119 |

Freshwater Theatre Press

# ALL RIGHTS RETAINED BY INDIVIDUAL AUTHORS

**Please note that Freshwater Theatre retains no rights to the following scripts. If you wish to produce any of the following plays, please contact the author directly for royalty information. Information to contact the authors precedes each script.**

Cover Illustration copyright Matt Black Studios.

*The more local something is, the more it is universal. – Joan Miro*

### *About Freshwater Theatre:*

We believe that art comes from a place. And we believe, unapologetically, that our place is one of the very best. We exist not only to create our own theater, but to facilitate and promote a vision of the Twin Cities as a major exporter of performing arts. We do beautiful, brave work here. This is an artistic community of revelation, innovation and pride. We have big dreams for Freshwater Theatre Company, and that includes this entire community of artists, individually and collectively.

Founded by the husband and wife team of Ben Layne and Ruth Virkus, with the help of fantastic colleagues and friends, Freshwater Theatre Company's motto is simple: we love good stories, told simply and told well. We believe that theatre can be transformative, revelatory, and educational, but we love it best when it's a good time, too. We like to entertain, and we promise a helluva ride.

We refuse to apologize or compromise. It's time to get serious, Twin Cities. This isn't flyover country. We're a coast, too. In fact, we have more coastline in Minnesota than anywhere else in the United States. The water is just fresher here.

Freshwater Theatre. We're in it for all of us.

Freshwater Theatre Press

*These plays, produced by Freshwater Theatre, originally premiered in September 2012 in Minneapolis, Minnesota, at the nimbus theater. They featured the following artists.*

### *Ebbing*
by Janet Bristow, directed by Anya Kremenetsky
Feat. Christine Sweet & Bill Studer

### *Second Wedding*
written & performed by Rachel Flynn*
directed by Jamil Jude

### *ENTRE'ACT No. 1*
curated & directed by Scot Moore*
Feat. Derek "Duck" Washington & Ariel Leaf*

### *homeWrecker*
by Anonymous, directed by Kyle Ross Thomas
Feat. Josef Buchel

### *ENTRE'ACT No. 2*
curated & directed by Scot Moore*
Feat. Denise Baker and Shannon Troy Jones

### *Does This Look Gay On Me?*
Co-created & performed by Ariel Leaf* &
Briana McNamara, directed by Emilia Allen
Feat. Lacey Zeiler*, V.O.: Rachel Flynn*

### *Pelican Girls* (1699)
by Richard Ballon, directed by Chris Garza
Feat. Aly Westberg & Jon Dahl

### *ENTRE'ACT No. 3*
curated and directed by Scot Moore*
Feat. John Leaf & Lacey Zeiler*

### *Schadenfreude*
by Jason Rainey, directed by Jamil Jude
Feat: Alexis Clarksean & Josef Buchel

Freshwater Theatre Press

V.O.: Rachel Flynn*, Brian Watson-Jones, & Sam Crnobrna

*I Would Never Live in a Social Democracy. The Lines Are Way Too Long*
by Valerie Borey, directed by Cassandra Snow
Feat. Peyton McCandless

*Poplin*
by Ruth Virkus*, directed by Cassandra Snow
Feat. Denise Baker, Jim Bitney, & Kari Elizabeth Kjeldseth

*ENTRE'ACT No. 4*
curated & directed by Scot Moore*
Feat. Rachel Flynn* and Derek "Duck" Washington

*Since the Kids are Gone*
by Michael Long, directed by Nora Sachs
Sound by Ted Moore
Feat. Shannon Troy Jones & Elizabeth Olson

*Scars*
by Greg Abbott, directed by John Zeiler*
Feat. Rachel Austin & John Leaf

*Waiting*
by Emily Arachtingi, directed by Scott Pakudaitis
Feat. Kari Elizabeth Kjeldseth

*ENTRE'ACT No. 5*
curated & directed by Scot Moore*
Feat. Rachel Flynn* & Rachel Austin

*A Small Play About Marriage*
by Jen Scott, directed by Chris Garza
Feat. Derek "Duck" Washington, Shannon Troy Jones, Aly Westberg, Jon Dahl, Alexis Clarksean, Elizabeth Olson, & Briana Patnode

*Denotes Freshwater Theatre Company Member

Better (or) Worse

## *EBBING*

by

**Janet M. Bristow**

**Oklahoma and South Dakota**

**405-844-3910**

**405-664-3077 (cell)**

**jbristow3@gmail.com**

**Web Site https://sites.google.com/site/janetmbristowplays/**

Growing up in the Midwest, Janet's first unforgettable theatrical experience was the televised play *The Fantasticks* on the Hallmark Hall of Fame. Janet then spent her adult years working, dramatically, in multiple careers within the field called "computers". Working in this technical field for so long in Washington, DC, Boston, New York City, Silicon Valley and Alaska did not diminish her love of the arts. In fact, she solved a worrying software problem while attending *Madame Butterfly* at Lincoln Center (her standing ovation for the performance was doubly enthusiastic). She became inspired to try playwriting by her New York actor, film-maker son, James Claude Bristow, adventurer husband, Jim Bristow, writer step-daughter, Katie Bristow. Her first play *Doc-Dir*, a comedy about a woman's efforts to get a medical diagnosis and her subsequent suggestions to improve doctors, appeared in *Best in 10* in 2011 at Carpenter Square in Oklahoma City, OK.

Freshwater Theatre Press

## CHARACTERS

Woman                  An assertive retirement-aged woman wearing a blouse with buttons and a fashionable baseball hat. She is more dramatic and free-wheeling than her husband.

Man                     A retirement-aged businessman who uses his business skills and demeanor to convince his wife.

## SETTING

Living room with chairs and a telephone.

## TIME

Modern day

## SYNOPSIS

A loving, feisty married couple is making and comparing retirement lists. She uses a pen and paper and he uses a laptop or Nook. Through their many years of marriage they have developed a playful way of communicating

MAN

Let's make a list.

WOMAN

Let's make deux lists (holds up 2 fingers).

MAN

Doesn't a list come before deux lists? (holds up one finger then 2 fingers)

WOMAN

No. I mean let's each make our own lists and then compare them. (as she writes on paper) "My Ebbing List".

MAN

What? What's "ebbing"?

WOMAN

It's *my* word for "retiring".

MAN

(Sighs as types on laptop)

My retirement list. You know instead of retiree *I'd* rather be called that CIA title. RED! Retired, extremely dangerous.

WOMAN

More like "Retired, extremely delusional".

MAN and WOMAN

(feverish typing and writing with occasional cross outs, laughs and exclamations, humming)

WOMAN

OK, what's on your list?

MAN

Easy access to fishing.

WOMAN

Mine is easy access to theatre and that's not the dollar movie.

MAN

Not much theatre (pronounced grandly) near my favorite fishing holes, gosh darn.

WOMAN

Well, fish in a big city river.

MAN

Can't eat them.

WOMAN

I don't want to eat them. Just go *out* there and dangle that pole.

MAN

Dangle? You want me to go away and dangle?

WOMAN

Well, isn't that half the reason you like fishing? Being alone... in nature and sunrises and all that baloney?

MAN

Me, hunter gatherer.

WOMAN

Great, go hunter gather in a city river and then release the polluted buggers.

MAN

I got it. I'll drop you at the theatre and then go dangle in any water around?

WOMAN

Perfect. No kids' fishing ponds though as people might think you're a pervert.

MAN

(logically summarizing tone)

Item 1 is city with theatre with river, lake, stream, pond nearby. Google Earth here I come

WOMAN

What's number two on your list?

MAN

Hunting.

WOMAN

Can't you get a video game where you kill things instead?

MAN

Not the same. No smells. Gotta be cold, wet, dirty, nasty, manly...

WOMAN

OK. Item 2. Place to kill Bambi.

MAN

Venison. Ummm. I'm hungry. Let's go get a Bahn Mi sandwich? We can pick up some Pho (pronounced Fa) for dinner at the same time.

WOMAN

(enthusiastically)

That's another item for the list. Vietnamese restaurant. (as she writes)

MAN

(types)

And German.

WOMAN

And Thai.

MAN

And a steak house.

WOMAN

And a French bistro.

MAN

And bar-b-que.

WOMAN

And Indian.

MAN

Our meals are like the food court at the United Nation.

WOMAN

We've become quite cosmopolitan, dear.

MAN

Ok but only big cities will have all those. Why don't you try cooking them yourself?

WOMAN

(graphically)

Why don't you try sticking that fishing pole...

MAN

Next item?

WOMAN

Romantic. Nice sunsets, trees, walks.

MAN

Ah. I've been meaning to talk to you. Let's donate our copies of the Kama Sutra and The Joy of Sex. To recover from that last position I needed 3 scotches.

WOMAN

I needed 2 pain killers. (pause, grimace, remembering) Ok we donate the Kama and the Joy but we still need romance.

MAN

I'll send you flowers once a month and we'll negotiate who's on top doing all the work.

WOMAN

OK. (as writes) Flowers and negotiate topping.

MAN

OK. What's your next item?

WOMAN

Want a beer? (as she gets up and starts to exit to kitchen)

MAN

Yea.

**WOMAN**

(mumbles while exiting) Red. Yeah we're Red. (screams from kitchen)Pick up the phone.

**MAN**

(looks back at kitchen, looks at phone, picks up intercom phone)

Screaming to pick up the phone? (shakes head)

**WOMAN**

(entering room and hands beer to MAN)

Screaming and phoning are not mutually exclusive. I brought you a LITE beer since you need to LIGHTEN UP.

**MAN**

I just don't understand why screaming to use the phone ... (shakes head) never mind. Next item.

**WOMAN**

(thoughtfully)

I wish we had visited places a long time ago so we wouldn't be going through all this now. We should have spent more time traveling.

**MAN**

So the kids shouldn't have played baseball, curling, luge, cheese rolling, toe wrestling? No pumpkin chunkin' and cage fighting so we could retire easier *40* years later?

**WOMAN**

Well, they went off all well-adjusted team players and we're left with (pause) just us.

**MAN**

Jeez. Next item.

WOMAN

What are you typing now?

MAN

Just adding the color graphics, foot notes and pivot tables for my list. (holds out keyboard to admire his technically enhanced retirement table)

WOMAN

(sarcastically)

Great you can transfer your former job skills to our list making.

MAN

Glad the skills I used as a Fortune 500 vice-president for 24 years are finally being appreciated.

WOMAN

We always appreciated you, dear, really. We just never knew what the hell you did.

MAN

Next item.

WOMAN

A community that is in line with my politics.

MAN

We've lived in this community for 20 years so why change now.

WOMAN

Because I am bursting my bra with all my stifling. PTA, stifle. Library, stifle. Lunch with the girls, stifle. Dinner with friends, stifle. I'm goin' blow big soon.

MAN

Didn't realize it was that big of a problem

WOMAN

(dramatically reacting)

I have vented in secret. I have taken out my revenge on restroom tampon machines!

I go in there and just give them a whack with my purse. Dented tampon machines everywhere in town.

MAN

(shakes head)

Correct political community. (types) What is it you'd like to do when retired?

WOMAN

Well, I don't want to just sit and watch TV or sit in the sun or cook all day. I want to be active and outdoors.

MAN

(proud of his idea)

You could hunt and fish.

WOMAN

(gives him a look)

I was thinking more of traveling.

MAN

I'll be traveling to my annual fishing in Alaska and duck hunting in South Dakota.

WOMAN

Now why didn't I think of going with you? (with a flourish) I want museums in Italy, theatre in London, river barge in France.

MAN

(makes a flying fishing movement)

Suppose I could throw a line off a luxury barge? (typing) Investigate and document all fish species in international waters. Do you have a current passport?

WOMAN

(Enthusiastically)

Will have now that I have a picture for it. That last picture you of me took is great.

MAN

Honey, they won't accept that picture. It all out of focus and blurry.

WOMAN

Hell. That's what I love about it! (pause) I love out of focus and blurry. I have no wrinkles. I look 30 years younger. (pause, thinking, looks at husband with hands on hips) You know its particularly cruel that a 65-year-old retired husband takes up photography. Stop pointing that thing at me.

MAN

That used to mean something else, sweet cheeks. (smiles, starts typing) Appendix 2a. Get all required paperwork completed.

WOMAN

How about a home that is convenient for kids to get to?

MAN AND WOMAN

(thinking, stop)

Naah.

WOMAN

I want a real house. I don't want to be a vagabond in a RV. I don't want to pretend I enjoy all the other displaced retired people.

MAN

OK, no RV but how about we just put some furniture and clothes in one of those pod thingies. (makes square gesture) Just move around the country. Six month lease here, a year there? You know, Pod people.

WOMAN

In the 1950s, Pod People were a race of nomadic, extraterrestrial parasites as I remember.

MAN

Redefine. We'll redefine the word. We'll be pioneers. The return of the Pod people, older, wiser, smarter, mobile, *retired*.

WOMAN

Rootless, exhausted, drifter. (pause) Hea, that's another definition of Red!

MAN

(making Jujitsu movements)

Ah, come on. We'll be like a tactical, mobile unit ready to strike out for fun and adventure.

WOMAN

(making arthritic movements)

Inflaming our arthritis. Packing, unpacking. Bending, lifting.

MAN

What's the matter, honey? Why are you so negative?

WOMAN

(pause) I'm scared. We're changing everything.

MAN

But you thrive on change. It innervates you. Primes you like a pump. (makes pumping arm movements)

WOMAN

But now I'm a grandmother. Not like when I was a bra burning woman's libber.

MAN

You can be a post-menopausal, 40C, AARP crusader for (pause) orthotics. (pause) With a programmable cane that changes color to match your outfit. Medicare-covered hair extensions?

Better (or) Worse

WOMAN

That reminds me. We have to seriously put my Optimum Food Pain calculation into effect.

MAN

What the hell was that again?

WOMAN

I compare food to my arthritis pain. To determine if I cook it that day. First I have to assign a food a value based upon the trouble it is to prepare. Ready to eat is +2, must peel -1, hard to cut -1, nutrition +3, easy to freeze +2 . Butternut squash is -1, -1, +3, +2 =3.

MAN

My kind of thinking. Food as a number.

WOMAN

(says slowly)

Now the pain points. Feel like a muscle car hit me (pause) and then backed up, -2, 1 Margarita, +1, 1 pain pill, +5, 1 pain pill and 1 Celebrex, +7. Now, if food preparation is greater 3 and pain is greater than 1, THEN and only then, (slowly) you can have roasted squash ravioli with goat cheese, onions and balsamic syrup. Ta da!

MAN

I think you have just created a web app! Call it (pause) Food Subdues Pain.

WOMAN

Sounds kind of S and M. (pause) Food Kneads Pain? Double entendre?

MAN

(typing into computer)

Interesting app. Hmmmm. My next item is better scheduling of our time.

WOMAN

What, what? You're the problem. I come in here ready to leave for dinner and you're having a web chat with our 5-year-old grandson explaining supply side economics. (in child's voice) Trickle down, Papa? (laughs) Supply slide. I want a supply slide! Then the time I had to take a crying Girl Scout home because you explained carbs and diabetes.

MAN

It needed to be done. Should be taught in schools. Honey, honey. It'll be OK. (stands and starts kissing around her face).

WOMAN

Oh, no you don't. Not that again. Kissing, a few drinks, music and by the next morning I've agreed to South Dakota. (insert any state that you want)

MAN

Great pheasant hunting.

WOMAN

Yea, how's the theatre season there?

MAN

(hugging her)

Growing, I would say definitely growing.

WOMAN

Lists, we're doing an ebbing list. I will not be bamboozled.

MAN

(plays with her buttons)

No way, honey.

WOMAN

I'm supposed to be the temptress. I'm supposed to bend *you* to *my* wishes.

MAN

Bend, bend away. (chuckles, lewdly)

WOMAN

(slowly) I've got it. (dramatically) Red; Ready, ebbing, contenders. (hold arms up in ROCKIE fashion)

MAN

R E C. That's wreck, dear. Don't think we want to call ourselves wrecks. How about Retired, energetic, defenders?

WOMAN

Oh, no, no. (laughing) Ready, ebbing, DEPEND (pause) ers?

MAN

(laughing as they walk off hand in hand)

I love you, Red.

End of play.

*Second Wedding*

*By Rachel Flynn*

dirtyflynn@gmail.com

When Rachel Flynn first arrived at the University of Minnesota, Morris she was going to do a double major in Psychology and Communications – that seemed the mature and responsible thing to do. But by the second quarter of her freshman year, she came to her senses and realized that being mature and responsible is not nearly as much fun as playing with the theatre kids, so she promptly changed her major to Theatre Arts – with a Management minor so as to at least keep up appearances of "maturity and responsibility."

After earning her B.A., Rachel served as Public Relations Associate at The Children's Theatre Company for about 6 years, is currently the Marketing Director of the History Theatre and has earned her Masters degree in Arts & Cultural Management from St. Mary's University of Minnesota. She has worked in various capacities with numerous theater companies including Swandive Theatre, Lake Harriet Players, La Vie Theatre, STL Productions, and Bloomington Civic Theatre. Ever the over-achiever, Rachel was in two shows in last summer's Fringe Festival: Knit One, Purl the Other, with Unfold the Sky Productions, and Rambler Family Ramblers Final Christmas Reunion Spectacular, withOAFTrax Productions. Rachel has been seen onstage with Freshwater in Table 12 and Dirty Girls Come Clean – A Festival, and recently hit the stage with Theatre in the Round for their production of Independence this January, Freshwater's Going Down on the Queen of Minneapolis.

Rachel's favorite roles include The Music Man (Marian), BLISS: Three One-Acts (various roles), Postcards from the Corn Palace (various roles), Tartuffe (Elmire), and Savage in Limbo (Denise Savage).

This is Rachel's first published script.

**Second Wedding** – approx 7 min.

My mom is getting married today. *Again.* I wasn't around for the first one – not even a twinkle in my parents' eyes, as they say. This time, I'm 14—actually, I'm 14 years, 7 days, and *[mental counting]* 13 hours and whatever minutes old. Just a couple more months and I will finally be done with 8th grade. Almost done with braces too – I'm *really* hoping Dr. Erickson will take them off in time for school photos next year!

Anyway, today is my moms' day, so my main duty is to smile for photos, and be sweet when people I barely know compliment me on how much I've grown and what a nice young lady I am. Most of these people are friends of the family, not actually family – I mean, not blood-relatives-family. But what I've learned from my moms' experience is that the family we choose – our friends – can be just as important as the family we're born into. None of my mom's brothers or sisters or my grandma or any of my cousins are at today's event. It sounds really dramatic and kind of tragic when I say it like that, but really, I'm used to it. And I'm okay because I have awesome friends. And so does my mom. Our surrogate families. Plus I still have plenty of contact with my grandma and aunts and uncles and great aunts and great uncles and cousins on my Dad's side so it's not like I'm completely without ties in this world.

My mom and dad got divorced when I was . . . well, I think I was about 4 when the paperwork actually happened? I don't remember too much about it, I was too young. Which I think is a good thing. I do remember having to stay with my dad's sister and her family for a little while when it was happening. I was completely uncomfortable because they are SUPER-Catholic, and I mean with a capital C. "Sometimes they think Pope John Paul is too liberal." I'm not entirely sure what that means, but when my mom says it she rolls her eyes and scoffs. And I've had to sit through enough Sunday masses and dinner conversations about politics with my dad's mom to know that you don't question the Pope. Unless you're the kind of Catholic who misses Latin mass and public floggings.

Needless to say, today's event is NOT happening in a church. My mom and dad got married in a Catholic church – they were both raised Catholic. Both the youngest of their families too – Mom has 5 siblings, Dad has 3.

My mom's journey with the church finally ended when she and my dad got divorced. Up until the end she tried *really hard* to be a Good Catholic, to follow all the rules so that her life would be what the Church promised her. When she asked for guidance from her priest she was told to pray harder. The divorce obliterated her faith in the Church – in *any* church – but not necessarily in "god." My dad still goes to church but he's switched to Unitarian – unless we're visiting my grandma in which case we still put on the appearance of being practicing Catholics. *[eye roll]*

Today's ceremony and reception are being held in the home of my moms' friends, which is a big, beautiful, old house that was built for hosting dinner parties. The hosts *love* to entertain – they have something like 12 full sets of china and I don't even know how many different linens and stuff – so today is right up their alley. The ceremony is being performed—er, conducted—or, "done" by my moms' friend Paula who is *way* into New Age stuff (which seems a lot like Native American and Druid stuff so it's weird that they call it "New" age). Anyway, this wedding ceremony – unlike any of the others ones I've ever been to – has zero mentions of Jesus. It's about souls finding each other and strengthening one another and sharing love with each other and with the people who surround them. It's really very lovely. Very *them*.

When today is done not much will have changed. I mean, the three of us have been living together as a family since before I started kindergarten. We're living the "Suburban Dream" in Eagan: 4-bedroom house, attached 2-car garage, finished basement, 3-season porch. We experimented with having a dog – "Worst mistake we ever made as a family" according to my mom. Marble is now living with a family that is taking good care of her. Before that, we experimented with having a couple of cats – But it didn't take long to discover that we're *really* allergic to cats. So they're now living with Sheila's mom and aunt in Pine Island. When I was 8 we went did the big Orlando vacation. We've done the long family road trip thing – in fact, this summer we're driving the Snackmobile all the way to Alaska. "The Snackmobile" is what we call our minivan. Yes. We have a minivan. (I'm pretty sure there's some sort of law requiring all residents of Eagan to own at least one minivan.) I think the only thing about our family that isn't very "normal" is that my mom quit her job at Kellogg's a few years ago to become a stand-up comedian. Not many people in Eagan can say that. Being a child of divorce certainly doesn't make me any less "normal" these days – when I was in sixth grade all three of my best friends' parents were divorced. Like many children of divorce, my mom has primary custody, but I get to spend Wednesday nights and weekends with my dad. Unlike most divorced families, my mom and dad still actually like each other. And we all still spend Christmas Eve together as a family – 10 years worth of pictures of our strangely-normal, normally-strange little family in front of our fireplace.

After today about the only thing that will be different is that my mom and Sheila – my moms – will wear matching rings, just simple yellow and white gold bands, inscribed with today's date. They don't get to file their taxes differently, or be covered on one another's health insurance. If something were to happen to either of them it would be up their siblings to tell the doctors what to do. In Sheila's case, her brother and sister are cool and they acknowledge us as a family. But if it were my mom, I'm not sure that her family would let Sheila in… That thought used to scare me. Like, what if something somehow happened to both my mom and my dad, would my next-of-kin let me stay with Sheila in my home? Now I'm less worried about it because I'm old enough to declare what I want and to put up a fight if anybody tries to make me go live with my dad's sister again. But still, there could be a fight. Do other kids have to worry about that?

Well, it's not something to worry about today. Plus, now I've got a house full of witnesses that I could call on should anybody ever try question who my mom and Sheila are to one another. They're life partners. They're happy. They're good together and good for one another. They argue and they laugh together. They kiss each other good night before falling asleep next to one another. They're raising a child (and doing a damn fine job if I do say so myself – which I do). They share a home: my mom mows the lawn and does the laundry, Sheila cleans the floors and handles the finances, I do the dusting. They're my moms. They're in it for the long haul. They are married.

Anyway, time for some more pictures. Fortunately the weather has cooperated and it's a beautiful April day. So we're heading out to the front yard, where it's a little less crowded, to snap some more photos of our strange little family.

*2012 marks 30 Years Together!*

Freshwater Theatre Press

## homeWrecker

**Please contact** info@freshwatertheatre.com **to obtain permission to reproduce this piece, as the author wishes to remain anonymous.**

*(probably at a bar- several drinks in- to a bartender or someone that is listening)*

He: She left it in the hotel room once. Sitting next to the empty martini glass with sugar still lingering on parts of the rim from her old fashioned sidecar. A drink she taught me to make just so I could order it correctly. I never made her drinks. Her wife did that. She didn't always take it off, I think mostly it was when we were fucking in strange hotel rooms that she would quickly remove it as a part of stripping down before laying before me to service her. She had to run back to the hotel later that night, with some excuse that I never heard.

She wasn't the first married woman I had been with or anything- all of the others took them off too. Mostly it was just when we would fuck. Never when we were out. Must have been an internal thing, huh? Not about other people knowing or seeing us together. Her with a giant rock on her finger- or a small one... depending. *(takes a shot)*

Both my maternal and paternal grandmothers had affairs. Dad's mom was fucking the neighbor on either side plus the *milkman*--no joke. The family ended up moving to a different neighborhood. My other grandmother's tryst began when he sold her family their house. That affair lasted seven years and didn't end until she left her husband- to marry the realtor instead. Now, those two are the only example of a happy couple I have in my family- together almost forty years. Maybe the infidelity runs in my veins. Genetically predisposed to wreck homes.

*(pause)*

Laying on my back, next to me a blissful-for-the-first-time in- who-knows-how-long woman still panting heavily, leg thrown over my sweaty knee peeking out from the rip in my jeans. I stare at the night-stand where her little silver, gold, or platinum cuff sits next to a condom wrapper and a full ashtray. She's supposed to be owned by someone else. That's what the institution is, right?- ownership. The man who **owns** his woman- she is property by law- the basis of marriage. Not this romantic white dress, open bar, cake fight supposed partner for life shitshow that it has been glorified to be. *(shot maybe)*

Then I fell in **love** with a married woman. I watched her decide that kissing me was something that she wanted to do. Something that was inevitable for us. We were in love before it even happened. *(pause)*

She started taking off her ring to fuck me- sliding it across the night-stand or the desk, the diamond scratching at the cheap fake wood. The clanky jingle of her two rings together started to excite me because I knew what was coming next. Then her rings were gone more often; I noticed because I wanted to forget. For the first time I wanted to forget that the person I was loving had ever been loved by anyone else- let alone that she was, *cuffed*. The ring disappeared after a while- I didn't have to remember. Not like I needed that to remember, it was always lurking behind the curtain. But we fell in love- so her collar came off. I like the way her bare fingers feel intertwind with mine. I would never put something between our skin when we're holding hands.

*(shot probably)*

Her husband saw us today- he walked right into where we were having lunch and saw the two of us together. I didn't flinch, hell I didn't even puff up my chest at first.*(shot- at this point he is drinking pure sarcasm)* Funny how big he needed to get, even with that contract to back him up. Then our carnal insticts took over- I stood to expand my wingspan, my gorilla shoulders squaring off as I walked out the door. Emotionally unchanged though- I was acting from internal impulse alone. People have been fucking the falicy of marriage for a long time- **way before** he walked into that restaraunt and ya know what? They'll keep doing it- no matter what cause that's just who we are.

    Animals. we're all just animals. And rings don't fit on paws very well man- they don't fit on paws.

## DO YOU THINK THIS LOOKS GAY ON ME?
*Created by Ariel Leaf and Bria McNamara*

Ariel Leaf

fishgirlariel@gmail.com

Ariel Leaf is a performer, writer, lighting designer, and director.

Along with Freshwater, she is a company member of 20% Theatre and the Footprints Collective. This year she will perform in Intrigue with Faye for 20% in January, Bohemian Flats with nimbus, design lights for The Gifted Program with Freshwater in April, perform/produce/AD the Vet Play Project with Footprints in the fall, and produce/perform in Stop Kiss in January 2014. She promises to still find time for her husband. *Does this look Gay on Me* is based on a series of real life conversations with Bria about their sexuality and marriages.

Briana McNamara has acted, Never.

As co-creator of "Does This Look Gay on Me," Briana sticks her neck out into acting in a very gutsy (and to her, VERY nerve wracking) way. Mrs McNamara did, in fact, get married on September 29th, thus adding a whole new element of stress, relevance, and dimension to the stylized portraiture of herself that is revealed in "Does This Look Gay on Me."

A long term advocate of GLBT rights, Briana is thrilled to be asked to participate in a production whose proceeds will benefit Minnesota For All Families, a cause she holds near and dear to her heart.

Mrs. McNamara would like to say THANK YOU to her husband Dan, to her close friend-confidant-and co-creator Ariel, Freshwater, to her single father who is more of a feminist then she is, and to the plethora of other folks that have supported and encouraged her through this amazing experience.

*Cast:*

BRIA: Bria McNamara
ARIEL: Ariel Leaf
JENNY: Lacey Zeiler

*Lights up. We are at the women's changing room in JC Penny. We see a woman dressed business casual at a counter on one side of the stage, folding a pile of clothes. She's wearing a name tag. The convention is that, while she's at the table, unless called to, she can't overheard the two women. In the center of the stage, near a door or wall (some sort of partition), ARIEL sits in a folding chair, a pile of clothes beside her. Beat. Beat. Then, from behind the partition...*

BRIA: oh HELL NO!

*Ariel looks up.*

ARIEL: Get out here.

BRIA: No. No. I'm taking it off.

ARIEL: Come on. Let me see.

*BRIA first pops here head around the partition, then emerges, flirting heavily.*

BRIA Hey baby... What do you think?

*She is wearing a sleeveless shirt, skirt or shorts and engineer boots*

Do you think this looks gay on me?

ARIEL: What?

BRIA: The shirt, the boots?

ARIEL: For fuck's sake...

BRIA: Hold on. Excuse me!

*The saleswoman looks up.*

Ummm....

*Looks at name tag*

Jenny? What do you think?

*She turns around. The woman looks at her appreciatively.*

JENNY: That fits you really well! I love the color.

ARIEL: See?

JENNY: I think there's a scarf in accessories that would look perfect with that.

BRIA: By all means.... (*Jenny exits*) See?

ARIEL: What? She confirmed it. That's totally hot. Do you feel sexy in it?

*BRIA shrugs noncommittally and moves around in front of the mirror.*

So it's a little butch. So the girls'll like it. What's wrong with that? I mean, it's fun sometimes, right?

Little flirtation, little "You want this but you can't have it?" Doesn't that feel sexy?

BRIA: On my HONEYMOON?

*ARIEL shrugs. Her attempt at humor clearly fell flat.*

ARIEL: Never mind.

*Jenny re-enters. She is carrying the scarf.*

BRIA: Thanks.

*She tries it on.*

JENNY: That is perfect.

*Bria goes to button the shirt.*

Don't button it all the way! Leave the top one undone. It's really attractive that way.

*From behind her, ARIEL raises an eyebrow at BRIA. BRIA blushes. Jenny blushes a little herself.*

Can I get you anything else right now?

*BRIA can't talk. ARIEL jumps in.*

ARIEL: No, we're good. Thanks.

*Jenny returns to the desk.*

I think you should get it anyway. For a night we go out or something.

BRIA: That would be so wrong! I can't show this to Dan and say "Honey, you don't mind that I spent some of our honeymoon money on a shirt that's going to make women look at my titties, do you?"

ARIEL: Trust me, men will look at them too.

*BRIA gives her a look.*

Wanna try it without the boots?

*Another look*

Ok, fine. Take it off.

*BRIA goes back behind the partition. After a moment.*

Are you still worried about it?

*No answer.*

Look, we're human right? So what if women still turn you on? Marriage is awesome and all, but that doesn't mean people stop being aroused. I'm sure when Dan sees a hot chick…

BRIA: What about you?

ARIEL: Me?

BRIA: Well don't you get all turned on when you see a hot chick?

ARIEL: Kinda. Not it the same way, but you know me. I'm just sboringly monogamous by nature. It's not that I don't look, or notice, it's just…abstract. It doesn't push my buttons. And it's never been about bodies for me, the same way it's never been about gender. I'm turned on by something more ephemeral that a great pair of tits. Not saying I don't appreciate them but…

BRIA: You never see someone, bite your lip and think "God, I want a piece of that."?

ARIEL: Maybe sometimes. I guess some of the FtM trannies in my show got me kinda hot… the fluidity, flexibility in the notion of gender gets me wet…

BRIA: See?

ARIEL: But I think what was sexy was their confidence. The amount of determination that went in to making themselves exactly who they wanted to be. THAT gives me a big fat boner.

*Bria comes out wearing something new, checks herself out.*

BRIA: I'm an immensely sexual human being. I love Dan more than anyone I ever have, but god, I still love looking at women.

*Runs her hands over herself*

Like when I saw that girl at the co-op... my throat goes dry, my mouth swells with saliva, my thighs tighten... I don't think that will ever go away.

*Jenny looks up, sees BRIA. She comes over.*

JENNY: Finally someone who looks GOOD in that!

*BRIA does. Jenny speaks in a quiet, confidential tone.*

All those ugly, flat chested soccer moms that come through here?

*She shudders dramatically*

Wait, let me adjust those straps darlin...

*She reaches out and adjusts the should strap. While her hands are on BRIA, BRIA throws a look at ARIEL. Ariel smiles. BRIA keeps her hands as far away from the other woman as possible, which isn't very far.*

There. Don't you think?

BRIA: (*Stammering*) Uh yeah... yeah, that looks awesome.

ARIEL: She'll take it.

JENNY: Great! Just bring it to me when she takes it off. I'll start a pile for you.

*Jenny goes back to the counter. Silence. BRIA checks herself out again.*

ARIEL: Are you going to be faithful?

BRIA: Of course!

ARIEL: So then what...?

BRIA: I don't see other men that way. Not in the "I want to fuck them" kind of way.

ARIEL: I guess. I never have either. I mean, when I was single I always looked at chicks much more sexually, men more.... I dunno... Intellectually?

*BRIA snorts*

BRIA: When have you ever been single?

ARIEL: Well...

*BRIA goes back behind the partition.*

I had an open relationship with Tony.

BRIA: I remember. That worked out GREAT, didn't it?

ARIEL: Shut up. It was his idea.

BRIA: Yeah, that never made sense to me. He didn't take advantage of it, did he?

ARIEL: Only when we tried having a thing with that couple. Some how he got obsessed with the idea he wasn't enough for me. I'm not totally sure why. He gave me a lot of different reasons, I was married so young so I must want to play the field, I'm gay so he must not fulfill all my sexual desires... In the end I think he was already dreaming of having sex with the ex-girlfriend he eventually left me to marry.

BRIA: So did that make a difference?

ARIEL: I guess. I mean, I did look at people sexually then. I had a awesome girlfriend... but that ended horribly. You remember.

BRIA: Was that the chick that dumped you?

ARIEL: No. That I could have handled. It was more like the fucking gay community dumped me. Let me tell you, nothing's more fun than being the only bisexual also dating a man in a room of hard core lesbians. They hated me. And I hated the whole thing. It was so nice to have sex with a woman again, to feel her muscles clench around my fingers... (*BRIA makes an appreciative sound*) but I felt guilty with both of them. That I wasn't giving them enough, that I didn't belong anywhere. I don't think I could do that again. Could you? I mean, if Dan wanted too?

BRIA: Could I fuck other women? Probably. But I have double standards.

*She emerges again*

I wouldn't be able to share him. I don't share my toys.

ARIEL: Ummm....

BRIA: Yeah, it's hideous.

*Goes back behind the partition.*

ARIEL: I guess I'm the reverse. I don't really think I'd ever go for it, but if John did? I mean, not a relationship, just a one night thing? I don't think I'd care. I just don't really care about sex.

BRIA: Don't tell John that...

ARIEL: Do you miss dating girls? Or just having sex with them?

BRIA: I never really had long term things. It wasn't that I didn't want to, or I didn't love them it just...never happened. But it wasn't just about sex, it was about power. Knowing how to crack her open...how to make her scream, hold her thighs open till she just can't handle it, pulling her hair and watching her eyes dilate....

ARIEL: I kinda miss being scared I won't get her off. Did I do this right? Should I try this? The insecurity was kinda a turn on. It's so automatic with boys. You look at them sideways and they come.

*BRIA comes back out.*

And I miss feeling part of a group. Having a family. I've always struggled with feeling like an outsider, and that was a family I really wanted to be part of.

BRIA: Come on. You're part of 20% theatre, you just did a whole Gender Queer show...

ARIEL: Yeah, but I didn't really feel like I belonged. Cause I'm married. To a man. I remember I got my T-shirt...

BRIA: Which one?

ARIEL: The one for the show? That said "I'm QUEER" on one side, and "Whatever the hell that means" on the other?

BRIA: That one's awesome!

ARIEL: Yeah, but I felt awkward wearing it. I liked wearing it when no one saw me. It made me feel proud. It felt right. But then when I wore it in the dressing room.... I felt like a fraud.

*Bria reaches for a pull over (she came out in a tank top) and puts it on.*

That's super cute.

BRIA: Yeah?

*She leans over in the mirror.*

It does show off my... assets.

*They both giggle. ARIEL catches JENNY watching.*

ARIEL: Get it.

*BRIA returns behind the partition. After a second she hands the tank top to ARIEL, who takes it to JENNY.*

JENNY: I'll add it to your things.

*ARIEL starts to walk away.*

JENNY: Um...

ARIEL: Yeah?

*Silence.*

ARIEL: I'm sorry, are we taking too long? Does someone else need the dressing room?

JENNY: No... no... you're fine.

ARIEL: Ok...

*Silence again. Eventually JENNY throws ARIEL an awkward smile and goes back to work. ARIEL goes back over to the chair. Silence.*

ARIEL: You ok?

BRIA: No.

*Silence.*

BRIA: I'm scared. I'm scared I'll always want women. I'm fucking scared that one day I'll wake up a lesbian and hurt my best friend.

ARIEL: Have you talked with Dan about it?

BRIA: Yeah. We're pretty open. He tries to laugh it off, to comfort me. He says "That's cool, as long as you're a lesbian who wants to have sex with me".

ARIEL: That's an awesome answer. He's an awesome guy.

*BRIA emerges.*

BRIA: Yeah but... I mean, I want to spend the rest of my life with Dan, but what I'm afraid of is not wanting to have sex with Dan for the rest of my life.

ARIEL: But you still want to marry him.

BRIA: I want to spend the rest of my life with him. I love him. I love that he gets me. I love that he scratches my back, that I can walk around naked in front of him, that he has a great ass...

ARIEL: So it's worth giving it a shot right?

BRIA: But I don't want to hurt him.

ARIEL: It sounds like he gets it. And that he loves you any way. That he's willing to try. That's fantastic.

BRIA: Yeah, he's pretty awesome.

*Looks at herself.*

Ok, I like this too.

ARIEL: Well, that's all the stuff we grabbed. You want to look around again?

BRIA: Hell no. I want a shot of Jameson and a Cider.

ARIEL: Sounds sweet to me. Take it off, and let's get out of here.

*BRIA goes back behind. ARIEL gathers up the rejects and brings them to JENNY.*

She's bringing one more thing out. These we don't want.

JENNY: Should I start ringing you up?

ARIEL: That'd be great.

*She does. BRIA emerges holding the last article and comes up to the counter.*

JENNY: that will be $52.47

*BRIA pays, JENNY puts it all in a bag.*

BRIA: Thanks for your help....

JENNY: No problem. You ladies have a great day.

*She exits. BRIA starts to fold up the receipt.*

ARIEL: What's that?

*They look closer.*

BRIA *(blushing)* I think that's her phone number.

*They stand there uncomfortable, torn between being pleased and embarrassed. Finally ARIEL puts her arm around BRIA and kisses her on the head.*

ARIEL: Well, old married lady or not, you'll always be sexy.

*They exit. Lights down.*

Freshwater Theatre Press

*Pelican Girls*

Richard Ballon

PO Box 1017

Amherst MA 01004

kissedbythemoon@yahoo.com

*Time and setting:*          *Fort Louis de la Mobile, Alabama 1699*

*Character:*               *Marie Saint-Chapelle   17 years old*

*Historical note: Mobile at this time was a French colony.*

*The set should be simple, a rough wooden table, a stool.*

We thought it may be an improvement to the orphanage where we worked eleven hour days in various trades for a gruel so grey it matched the colors of the eyes of the workmen. The Mother Superior put my name in the lottery for brides of New France. I had never seen a ship and imagined it solid as an island. It was teetering with supplies, cattle and the smell of something rotten.

Oh, we the women were protected like the most treasured wheat. We were locked aboard ship, in a cabin, elbow to knee and let out to air, where the sailors gawked at us. How those men smelled like low tide, and panted and pawed themselves. Once we had to throw one overboard to cool him down, but he missed the rope and was heaved over a wave and disappeared from sight. A long time we left the rope to wriggle in the water like an eel and even left it trailing.

When I stepped off the boat, finally to land, and saw all the gentlemen, hats in hand, their clothes a style of a decade ago with long curls greased with a bit of fat. The light glinted off one man's rings so I barely noticed he was missing a big tooth, when he smiled, spoke to us, and his words whistled; his rough French, sweet as wine.

Each of us had been assigned a man, and when mine approached, I thought, No. I didn't travel this far to be courted by a toad. The man who waddled toward me had fat hands, greenish stubble on his pockmarked face and a line of grease across his wrists where his frayed shirt cut into his wrist.

I turned my head and caught Mary's man, Jean Marie, who was looking at me like a cow eying some clover. He fell in love with my mouth, he told me later. The toad tried not to notice us looking at each other but the pull was so strong, he shuffled in front of Mary, and switched their place. Mary's mouth opened like a fish and the toad told her, quiet like, with a voice that purred warm, Mary you can do the fishing, which was in contrast to a whoop of glee as Jean Marie took my hands. Mary shone her shy eyes at the toad and they warmed his, and a new hearth was lain with a fire between them, while mine were ablaze as Jean Marie leaned in, the twinkle in his eye flashing like the mother of pearl buttons by the froth of his beard.

He reminded me of my uncle Jean Pierre who was said to have a wife for each day of the week, but that was all talk, 'cause his only wife, Madeline clung to him like he was some puppy who might run amuck.

Papers had been arranged before we arrived, so the clerk, seeing what common eyes could see, crossed out Mary's name, replaced it with my own and only then, above his head, did I see the river, dark as a snake's belly, undulating through a forest of trees the same shade of sluggish green. We were in New France.

The grasp of Jean Marie was strong, and the shape of his arm like the arm of a fancy chair, and one I longed to sit on. Flushed by the fresh air, with wobbly legs from the boat, he swept me up with a whoop off the ground as the men cheered. The other girls walked with eyes cast down like a line of nuns to prayer to the cabin that would house us until the morning opened the flower of our new life.

He hoisted me on his back like a child on a hobby horse and ran with me to the tavern where another cheer broke free. I quaffed two beers and don't remember how I found my face in a pillow that smelled of wood smoke and another woman's perfume. I jostled and tried to make him stop the journey of my own desire which traveled across my breast and thighs like a sailor swimming mad for the shore that lay between my two legs.

When the morning light flooded the room, I could see the tattered blanket, snowshoes and rough rope in the loft and a hearth all bare and cold. I was told to dress, it was my wedding day, the lucky lass I am, and I donned my wedding weeds and braided my hair away from a face flushed with what had been; stepped where the others stood on the steps of the church, but they wouldn't look at me.

The curt nod of the priest told us all to enter where the men stood rubbed clean and full of a strange musk scent, so stiff, so tall, like bowling pins soon to be knocked into a proper life. But among them there was a gap, like a mad laugh, where I was directed to stand.

I was wed to the gap. I said the words, but to no one, but I noticed each man in the church mouthed the words to me, married to my emptiness, sanctified. I saw the true meaning of it all. I was the whore the village was marrying and through this rite the men could not sin because in sickness and in health I would have them all and I was theirs to have. Like all things ordained. My Man was a trapper and had left in the rust of dawn to venture north to his traps and his squaw. And Mary's husband, the man who could have been mine, flashed happy eyes at me, like the jewel of a life that could have been my own.

Freshwater Theatre Press

**Schadenfreude**

by

Jason Rainey

Jason Rainey is a graduate of the University of North Texas and a member of ScriptWorks in Austin. His work has been commissioned, presented, or produced by ScriptWorks, Last Frontier Theatre Conference (Valdez, AK), Penobscot Theatre (Bangor, ME), Daedalus Theatre (Columbus), Mildred's Umbrella (Houston), Sound Plays, Texas Dramatist Playwriting Series, and Punchkin Rep in Austin. He has twice directed his own short plays at Austin's FronteraFest, receiving a Best of Fest citation for *Schadenfreude* in 2010. Punchkin Rep will produce Jason's full-length play, *Gods and Idols*, at FronteraFest in early 2013.

Contact information:

Jason Rainey

jasonrainey31@yahoo.com

*[As the lights rise, a large butcher paper banner is visible at the back of the stage. The letters are in black on a white background, with red trim.*

*The banner reads: WELCOME BHS ALUMS*

*JEFF, a genial man in his late 20s, stands stage left, a beer in hand. He wears a respectable suit and frequently looks at his phone. After a few moments, LORI enters stage right. She is also in her late 20s, holding a cocktail, with a purse flung over her shoulder. She gives the initial impression that she might be intoxicated. She wears an evening formal, something perhaps more suitable for a prom night, and one that doesn't fit quite properly. LORI glances around unknowingly until she spots JEFF, whom she recognizes.]*

LORI

Hey, aren't you Mr. Homecoming Queen?

JEFF

Sorry…

LORI

Yes, it's you. You…

JEFF

No, I didn't go to school here.

LORI

No, no. You married Janet, the Homecoming Queen.

JEFF

Janet Latham. Yes.

LORI

I'm Misses… Miz … no, Misses Homecoming King. I married Trent.

JEFF

Oh, so you must be Lori.

LORI

Yes, and you're Jeff, right?

JEFF

Yes.

LORI

It's good to finally meet you.

JEFF

You, too. (*They shake hands.*) They're going to take a photo of the four of us for the alumni magazine.

LORI

That's right. Wouldn't miss it.

JEFF

*(looks off stage as if trying to locate his wife)*

Have you met Janet yet?

LORI

Oh, yes. When we first got here. I think you were in the john or something. (*She pulls out a program from her purse.*) Did you get one… Have you seen this? (*She opens the program to a specific picture.*) Look at them. Ten years ago. She is a lovely, lovely girl. As photogenic as she is, this picture does her no justice. She is just lovely.

JEFF

Thanks. Yes, Janet's really been looking forward to tonight.

LORI

*(after a pause; wistful)*

Ten years.

JEFF

Did you know Janet in high school?

LORI

No, I didn't go to school here. I met Trent in college. Did you…

JEFF

No, Janet and I met at my cousin's wedding, actually.

LORI

Oh, that's lovely.

JEFF

How long have you two…

LORI

Since college. You? You got any kids?

JEFF

Just a little over a year now. No kids yet.

LORI

We have two children. I have some school pictures here… This is our son, Hunter. And this is our daughter… Gatherer. (*beat*) I'm kidding. I'm just kidding. That's Virginia, named after Trent's mother.

JEFF

They're good-looking kids. Hunter looks like his dad.

LORI

Thanks. Oh, so you've met Trent? You said that my son looks like him…

JEFF

From the picture in the program…

LORI

Ah. (*She puts the pictures back in her purse.*) So, you know they're going to dance, right?

(JEFF *nods.* LORI *points at a space behind the audience. They will reference this point whenever acknowledging the action taking place off stage. It will also be clear that the action taking place off stage is at a considerable distance – with* JEFF *and* LORI *sometimes straining to see – as they are in the far rear of the banquet hall.*)

LORI

After this lady gets on with it, they're going to have a little walk down memory lane. The old Homecoming King and Queen…dancing together again.

JEFF

Yes, that's what Janet said.

LORI

Do you find that it's a little odd?

JEFF

How do you mean?

LORI

I mean, I'm his wife, and no one's dancing with me. (*She laughs nervously.*)

JEFF

Well, we went to my 10-year reunion last year, and they did something similar.

LORI

Oh, you were the Homecoming King?

JEFF

No.

LORI

Me neither. Well, I wasn't the Queen, I mean.

JEFF

(*cheery*)

I don't think they'll dance for very long. In fact, I think we're expected to jump in and finish the dance with everybody else.

LORI

Maybe you and I should dance while they're dancing, see how everybody likes that. (*She waits for a reaction; none comes.*) So, they were really quite the couple in high school, weren't they? Together for so long. Why do you think they broke it off?

JEFF

Well, that was high school, I guess. They went their separate ways.

LORI

Well, they did try again for a little while in college. Did you know that?

JEFF

No. Like I said, Janet and I met…

LORI

That's right, that's right. Only a year ago. (*She takes a drink.*) Well, Trent and I broke up for a while our sophomore year, and he sent Janet an email or something. I forget. Wanted to get back together.

JEFF

She never told me that.

LORI

Yeah, well, it was separation anxiety or something, I'm sure. Look, would you mind getting me another drink?

JEFF

Oh. No, not at all. What do you want?

LORI

Surprise me, Jeffrey.

(*JEFF exits stage right, while LORI looks ahead, listening to presentations. She opens the program again, trying to find a schedule so she can follow along.*)

LORI

What are we up to? "Most Changed Since High School." Well, that won't be my husband. (*She strains to see.*) Who'd they give it to?

(*JEFF returns with a drink and hands it to LORI.*)

LORI

Hey, thanks. Jeff, you've got to see this. They just gave the "Most Changed Since High School" award to that woman.

JEFF

Do you want to move closer?

LORI

God no. It's more fun back here in the shadows. Do you see her? I swear it's a cruel joke. (*She takes a drink.*)

JEFF

Oh, yeah. I think that's Priscilla. Met her earlier.

LORI

I'm guessing it's really the "Most Quadrupled Since High School" award. It's just cruel to give her this.

JEFF

(*taken aback but trying to remain sensible*)

I think Janet was telling me that she's a lawyer now. Something completely unexpected.

LORI

Well, when the rest of her ass gets to the stage, we can see who gets the next award. Jesus! (*She looks at the program.*) What's next? Oh, my favorite. "Most Inspirational Alum." Oh, I bet I know who wins this…yep, I was right.

JEFF

Do you know him?

LORI

Todd Sothern. One of Trent's best friends back in high school. He was burned in a house fire…like 40 percent of his body.

JEFF

God, that's awful.

LORI

Now he's in med school. He's such an *inspiration*. Hold on, I want to hear what he says. You know, who are these assholes who "regret nothing because it's made me the person I am today"? What is that?

JEFF

I'm sure it's a way to cope…

LORI

Well, I think he's full of shit. Regrets nothing? (*loudly*) How about smoking in bed, Todd!

JEFF

Lori, you're being a little loud.

LORI

Oh, oh, you're right. Sorry. Shh….

JEFF

Actually, I need to go and see…

LORI

Who do you need to see, Jeffrey? You're a fish out of water here, just like me. (*She takes him arm in arm.*) Besides, we've got to stick together for that photo, right?

JEFF

(*reluctant*)

I guess you're right.

LORI

OK, we're up to "Traveled Farthest to Get Here." Well, again, that won't be my husband. We bought his parent's house last year. Where do you live, by the way?

JEFF

We live in Phoenix.

LORI

Ah. (*She wiggles her drink.*) Say, how much do I owe you?

JEFF

Don't worry about it.

LORI

Oh, that's very, very sweet, Jeffrey. (*She takes another drink.*) They had an open bar at my reunion. Couple of months back over the summer.

JEFF

Oh. How was that?

LORI

No clue. I didn't go. I had a friend who… (*She laughs.*) No, that would have been a disaster.

JEFF

So, do you and Trent keep up with many of his friends from high school?

LORI

Most of them moved away. I think he's on Facebook every once in a while… Trent's always on that god damn computer, so he's… Hey, what do you do for a living? No, let me guess.

JEFF

I just got…

LORI

No, I want to guess. I'm very, very good at this. (*She surveys him.*) You work in insurance.

JEFF

I do, in fact. How did…

LORI

I'm very, very good at this. You're probably in management.

JEFF

I was just promoted to office manager.

LORI

Middle management. (*beat*) Well, you're young.

JEFF

Neat trick. And what do you do? No, it's my turn to guess.

LORI

You'll never guess. I've worked at a nursing home for two years now. It's the second most depressing thing I will ever do.

JEFF

What's the first?

LORI

I'm sure something'll come along.

JEFF

Hey, can I see the program? I think there's a video coming up. Janet submitted some old pictures.

LORI

That's right. Trent and his mother were going through old photo albums a few weeks ago. Trent playing lacrosse. Trent at the lock-in. And, of course, Trent and Janet in several lovely poses.

*(The lights dim a bit, as the video begins off stage. JEFF AND LORI begin to whisper their dialogue, but soon LORI is talking at full volume.)*

LORI

It's strange to be so disconnected from this, isn't it? It's like watching a soap opera in Spanish. I get the gist of it, but ultimately I just don't care.

JEFF

I love seeing the hairstyles.

LORI

I wonder how much money goes into an event like this. And this video. *(in a knowingly phony self-righteous tone)* I'd hate to think that there are kids without textbooks…

JEFF

Lori, you know, I think this is just one of those times when you have to be an observer as opposed to…

LORI

Hey, don't start lecturing me. I'm just saying that this might be the most colossal waste of time and money I've ever seen.

JEFF

It's just a fun night. One night.

LORI

One night for you maybe. You live in Phoenix! *(Her anger growing, she looks back towards the banner and runs towards it. JEFF follows.)* I mean, look at this banner. "Welcome BHS alums!" What about wives? And husbands?

JEFF

I think it's implied.

LORI

No, it's insulting! (*She moves towards banner to pull it down.*)

JEFF

What are you doing? Stop!

LORI

This is an outrage!

JEFF

Jesus, Lori. Stop that! (*He grabs her and pulls her away from the banner before she can tear it down.*) Someone's going to see you.

LORI

I don't care!

JEFF

Lori, this is just one night. About your husband, about my wife, about their friends, about their life…

LORI

It was his life before he met me. It doesn't count!

(*LORI steps away from the banner, angry, her ego bruised. She drains her drink and walks back to the front of the stage. JEFF, confused and a little frightened, follows. Desperate to get her mind off of the night, he changes topics.*)

JEFF

So, tell me about your kids.

LORI

What do you want to know?

JEFF

They're your children. I'm sure you have lots to brag about.

## LORI

Well, Jenny...that's what we call Virginia, she's our oldest. We had her three months after our wedding. You do the math. She's named after Trent's mother, she looks like Trent's mother...so needless to say, she's the apple of her father's eye. And to top it off, now she's getting her period. Eight years old and she's getting her period! Can you imagine that? They say it's the hormones in the milk or the pollution in the air, I don't know. But now, once a month, she turns into the biggest bitch this side of her grandmother, and I alone have to bear the brunt of it. Trent's oblivious because she's his little angel. To him, she's just St. Virginia of the Golden Maxipad!

*(The lights return to full power as the video ends.)*

## LORI

Oh, the video's over. I guess it's time for the big dance.

## JEFF

*(looking through program)*

No, it looks like there are a few more awards to hand out.

*(JEFF now takes the attitude of an inquisitive reporter, one who senses that things don't add up.)*

## JEFF

So, I'm a little confused. You said that you and Trent broke up in college...your sophomore year, right? But your daughter's eight.

## LORI

When Trent got back together with Janet...that's when I found out I was pregnant, and he came back. We got married, I had my daughter, and I...

## JEFF

You dropped out of college.

## LORI

And then we had Hunter almost immediately after Jenny. And now we're...where we are.

JEFF

So, you said that they got back together for a while? Janet and your husband.

LORI

Yes, it was in college. He flew out to see her.

JEFF

But he, *they*, didn't know you were pregnant, did they?

LORI

Look, this is stupid. I think I need another drink. (*She cups her hand over her mouth.*) Or maybe a breath mint.

JEFF

No, I want to know. He goes to see Janet and then you find out that you're pregnant, and then what? He comes back right away?

LORI

Yeah, that sounds about right. Jeffrey, you are a quick study.

JEFF

But you said that your daughter was born three months after your wedding. Most people who have – and pardon the expression – "shotgun weddings"…

(*LORI interrupts with loud laughter. She pantomimes loading a shotgun and firing it. She laughs some more.*)

LORI

Shotgun wedding! Is that an insurance phrase? From the 1920s!

JEFF

Most people who have weddings because they're pregnant get married right away. But you waited until you were six months pregnant.

LORI

You know, what's the point? Why are you suddenly so interested?

JEFF

I want to know why it took so long for you to get married. Why didn't Trent just come back…

LORI

No, what you want to know…

JEFF

I want to know…

LORI

What you want to know is what your wife knew and when she knew it. And how long it took her to stop fucking the father of my child.

JEFF

Well, I'm sure that once she found out… I'm sure they weren't whooping it up, having a great time while you were pregnant and dropping out of college.

LORI

No, I don't think that was their plan.

JEFF

What does that mean?

(LORI *walks back towards the banner.*)

JEFF

Don't try pulling that down again!

LORI

I just need some space. Jesus, how much longer till this dance so I can get out of here?

JEFF

(*looking out*)

Trent's making a speech right now. Maybe you should come listen. (LORI *waves him off.*) Something about the lacrosse championship.

LORI

(*chortles*)

Lacrosse!

JEFF

He's toasting his teammates.

(*From the back, LORI raises her glass mockingly. She walks back towards JEFF.*)

LORI

I have to give it to Trent. He's a natural with a microphone. Very popular at weddings. I could never do that.

JEFF

You mean give speeches? Toasts? I'm a member of, um… Well, I'm terrible at speaking in front of people, too, so I joined this group called SpeakEasy, it helps you with your confidence. Anyway, it's helped me a lot. I gave a really good toast at our wedding, and then I've made a couple of presentations at corporate.

LORI

(*sincere*)

That's really great.

JEFF

Yeah, it's, you know, something you might consider…

LORI

(*abruptly*)

They sent me money for an abortion.

JEFF

What?

LORI

Trent and Janet sent me a 500-dollar check, with a lovely note from your dear wife, explaining that they were in love and that, for my sake, it would probably be best if I got an abortion.

JEFF

(*long pause*)

Maybe he forced her…

LORI

Maybe. But all I know is that the check was from her account, signed by her, accompanied by her letter. He even enrolled at her college.

JEFF

But you had Virginia. You got married…

LORI

It became pretty clear that I was going to go through with the pregnancy. And when it comes to guilt trips, Trent's mother is a cruise director.

JEFF

So he finally came home…

LORI

Months later…

JEFF

And you got married.

LORI

Isn't it wonderful?

JEFF

(*startled by something from off stage*)

Oh my god, now he's toasting *her*!

LORI

*(raises glass)*

Champagne wishes…!

*(JEFF and LORI stand, listening to the toast off stage. LORI's expression is one of bitterness that slowly fades to blankness. JEFF, absorbing everything, is horrified.)*

LORI

Well, that was code for, "Janet, I'd like to meet up with you at the Motel 6 later."

JEFF

Wait a minute! Holy shit!

LORI

What's got your dander up?

JEFF

Let me see that picture of your daughter. That school picture you showed me!

LORI

Okay, okay. Simmer down, middle manager.

*(She hands him the picture and after he looks at it, he throws his head back, mouth agape, in full disbelief.)*

LORI

Sudden case of narcolepsy, mister?

JEFF

Virginia *Janet* Miller?

LORI

Such a dignified name for an eight-year-old on the rag, don't you think?

JEFF

How could you…? Why in the hell would you name her that?

LORI

Like I had a choice!

JEFF

Did the five hundred go towards naming rights?

LORI

I ought to slap the fuck out of you.

JEFF

It's your daughter's name! And you name her after the two women you despise the most! What is your problem? What, you were so relieved to have him back, you'd do anything to keep him?

*(Composing herself, LORI walks over to him, her arm outstretched as if to shake hands.)*

LORI

Jeff, it's a been a real, real pleasure meeting you.

JEFF

No, no. You can drop the debutante act. You've been dumping this…*shit*…on me all night. You can't just walk away.

LORI

Well, I'm afraid I have to freshen up a bit, get ready to dance with my husband. Once he's done with your wife, of course. *(beat)* Just like old times.

JEFF

*(looks off stage; a bit frantic)*

Hey, look! The principal's making a few comments, and then Trent and Janet are going to have their dance. *(pause)* I want you to… Look, we don't have a lot of time. We just need to *do* something.

LORI

What are you talking about?

JEFF

You've been telling me these things about them that…honestly, I thought you were just some sad, crazy drunk…but I believe what you've said is true. I think maybe it's just time to get a little…I don't know…

LORI

Revenge?

JEFF

Yeah. Revenge. I'm suddenly feeling the need to make a toast of my own. I told you I've gotten really good.

LORI

I don't want any part…

JEFF

Look, I'm not talking about rigging pig's blood in the rafters. Just something…maybe a little embarrassing for them when they take the dance floor.

*(LORI opens the program one last time, staring at the picture of the old flames.)*

LORI

Okay. What do you want to do?

JEFF

I have a plan.

*(JEFF takes LORI by the hand and leads her off stage as the lights fade.)*

Freshwater Theatre Press

**I would never live in a social democracy. The lines are way too long.**

Valerie Borey

3744 Park Ave S

Minneapolis, MN 55407

612 922 9114

vborey@hotmail.com

*Character:* Diana, a virtuous and earnest maiden

*Setting: Ideally something classically romantic:*

*velvet, rose petals and soft white taffeta.*

DIANA

Will I marry you?

Will I marry you?

This is my song of love

These are the words I give to you

These words represent my mind, my body, my soul

You ask, will I marry you?

My answer is this:

I will.

I do.

I am yours.

When you hold me, I am yours.

Shhh. Let me speak frankly to you.

When I kiss you, when I bear your child, when we bury our parents, I am yours.

When you lose your job or make love to me, when we take

out a home equity loan, when we go to our kids' dance

recitals, I am yours.

When you stay out too late drinking, even though I

asked you not to and you did it anyways and almost

missed my sister's wedding, I am yours.

When you cry on my shoulder because your best friend

committed suicide, when you buy me roses on Valentine's

Day,

When you bring home gonorrhea, and deny it, or get a

confused look on your face and insist it must have been

the toilet seat in a public restroom,

When your sister gives our baby hand-me-down clothes as

a birthday present because she thinks I'm not good

enough for you and she wants me to know it but still

wants to get credit for giving something,

When you sigh in the kitchen because I forgot to clean

up after I spilled the sugar and left the teaspoon out,

And your parents call you at work because they don't

want to call at home on the chance that I'll answer the
telephone and they'll have to make small talk with me,
and you get the call that I'm in the emergency room and
you stop off at Taco Bell first because you haven't
eaten dinner yet,

When everything you say, every look you give me, every
muscle in your body tells me that I give you the
heebiejeebies,

When my mother moves in because she's gone blind and
you keep moving the furniture around on her,

When you say we don't have enough money saved up for a
vacation, but show up with a projection screen tv,

When you act like an asshole so my friends don't want
to come over anymore,

When you inappropriately touch the child I accidentally
had in high school before I met you,

When you tell me that I'm not attractive to you

anymore, that I'm too fat, that I'm too lazy, that I

always tell the same stories over and over again,

I am yours, darling. I am yours.

Because I really like that dress in the window: the one

with the creeping lace and pearl buttons and the train

that glides so elegantly on the floor. And I want my

hair done professionally, and I want my father to cry

when he walks me down the aisle, because he's never

really noticed me much and just once I would like to

have a party that's all about me. And I will spend

those first weeks wishing that you loved me as much as

I love you.

Oh, I know that all that's just temporary, short term.

In a few months, all the excitement will die down and

after a year or two people will start making nasty

little comments about me still having all the wedding

photos up in my cubicle at work. And I will stop

saying, "My HUSBAND this and my HUSBAND that, and the

other day, my HUSBAND.."

But it's okay, because I'll be pregnant by then anyways

and it'll be all about the baby and what kind of

diapers to use and whether or not listening to music in

vitro is good for brain development. By then, it won't

really matter if you're around or not, because mainly

I'll just need your health insurance and for you to

show up at one or two key events and look like you

care, even if you don't, even if you think we should

have waited a couple more years before starting a

family, and even though you actually had the nerve to

ask me if it was yours.

Because when the babies are grown and I'm re-entering

the workforce at minimum wage, I'll depend on you and

the two or three warm words you throw at me a year to

make me feel more special than the homeless lady I sit

next to on the bus every day. I will sleep on the couch

and get drunk every night and cold-call old friends

from high-school to reminisce about the good old days.

And by then I'll think I'm too old to leave you, too

tired to be on my own, and now that I have bladder

control issues, I can't imagine initiating sex with anyone else, and after all, there's your 401K and retirement will be coming up soon enough as it is and I don't want to be alone when I get old, stuck in section 8 housing and already decomposing when they find me weeks later.

So, yes, I'll marry you. I love you deeply, or at least what you represent to me. I give myself to you, body, soul, and mind. For better or for worse, in sickness and in health. I do.

And your ex- Ilka- can suck it when she finds out that you chose me. I won.

*Poplin*

By Ruth Virkus

ruth@freshwatertheatre.com

A National Merit Scholarship recipient who graduated with honors from the University of Minnesota Morris with degrees in history and theatre, Ruth Virkus is a founding member and co-artistic director of Freshwater Theatre. She is also a company member with 20% Theatre Company, Twin Cities.

Ruth has written or co-written many produced plays. Her first solo writing endeavor, *Preferred by Discreet Women Everywhere*, eventually begat a companion piece entitled *10:00 Bistro Caprice*, which was featured in The Fresh Five with 20% Theatre Company in January of 2010. Other works include *Table 12: A Play at a Wedding*, and *Desperation Panties*.

Ruth recently produced and curated Freshwater's *Dirty Girls Come Clean: The Return*, also directing a couple of the pieces in the fest, which raised over $2000 for Dress for Success Twin Cities, was recently onstage in Walking Shadow Theatre Company's production of An Ideal Husband and wrote and produced going *Down on the Queen of Minneapolis* for the 2012 MN Fringe.

During the day, Ruth happily works as a Property Manager for MSP Commercial, a real estate development firm based in Eagan, MN. In what spare time she has, she cooks a lot, makes bread and feeds it to people. Forcibly, if necessary.

## *Poplin*

Lavinia Williams
Minnie Erickson
Mr. Ohman


*The Bragg General Store in Ogilvie, Minnesota.  September of 1903.*

*Mr. Ohman+ is behind the counter, counting the eggs MINNIE has brought in.  MINNIE is a substantial lady, and clearly a woman of action.  She's made an effort to clean up for a trip to town, but she's gloveless and hatless, and not in her Sunday best.  One gets the sense she took off her apron, washed her face and hands, tucked in a few stray hairs, and called it good.*

MR OHLMAN
This isn't your usual day, Minnie!

MINNIE
I brought in the eggs on a Wednesday as an excuse to bring your Missus some baby things I won't miss, and an extra loaf from my last baking.  How are she and the new one?

MR OHMAN
She's tired, and he's loud for a tiny thing.  They're well.  She'll be sorry to miss you.

MINNIE
I'm so glad to hear it.  Give Beth my best.  Don't bother to count- I brought in three dozen there, all fresh and whole.  *(now all business)* Eleven cents a dozen, Mr. Ohman?

MR. OHMAN
10 cents.

MINNIE
I could have sworn it was eleven.

MR OHMAN
It's been a dime for the last year, Mrs. Erickson.

MINNIE
Ah, well- time for an increase, then.  Nothing else in here is selling for less than it did last year.  I can't see why inflation doesn't go both ways.

MR OHMAN
*(jovially)* Ten cents is still fair market, but it was a good effort.

MINNIE
If you take those three cents and deduct it from the price of your fabric, I'll be satisfied with my bargaining skills.

*MR OHMAN laughs. At that moment, LAVINIA enters. In contrast to MINNIE, she's gloved, with a fashionable hat, and an air of quiet.*

MR OHMAN
Mrs. Williams! It's not your usual day, either!

MINNIE
Oh, don't you look lovely, Mrs. Williams! *(the sight of the well put together Lavinia reminds her, and her hands fly to her head. Her chagrin is good natured)* My hat. I forgot my hat, again. Oof. You'll forgive me; I'm rarely fit for polite company.

LAVINIA
You're just as respectable without your hat, Mrs. Erickson. You look very well.

MINNIE
Oh, such polite fiction. At least I'm not shedding hayseed on you!

LAVINIA
I assure you-

MINNIE
You always look so elegant. You make one feel like a gargoyle sat next to a Gibson Girl.

LAVINIA
*(uncomfortably)* That's a very kind-

MINNIE
I'm too busy to be bothered, and it shows. Not to say that you're not as busy as I- I would imagine a banker's wife has a lot of- and you are so active in the church!

LAVINIA
Yes, I-

MINNIE
Oh, we missed you last week at services! I hope your young Robert is feeling better, I heard he had a bad summer cold-

*(she pauses)*

Well, that was just terribly forward and rude. I haven't let you finish a sentence, Mrs. Williams.

LAVINIA
*(smiles)* I'm glad to think we can be informal with each other, like real friends. Friends may use first names. Lavinia.

MINNIE
Minnie, of course. Oh, you *are* a lady.

MR OHMAN
Your thirty cents, Mrs. Erickson?

MINNIE
Oh, don't bother counting it out, I'm just going to spend it. Lavinia! If you have a moment, lend me your good taste.

LAVINIA
I'm intrigued!

MINNIE
My best dress isn't three years old, but I've gotten a bit stout for it, sadly. *(examining LAVINIA'S dress)* That's such fine fabric. You didn't get that poplin here, did you now? My apologies, Mr. Ohman.

LAVINIA
My husband brought it back from Minneapolis, as a gift.

MINNIE
*(sighs)* I thought so. I'd go down the street to the Dry Goods store, but I can get a third more yardage here for the same price, and I can't see spending what I don't have to. Arnie says it's up to me, but he says that about anything that doesn't moo.

LAVINIA
Mr. Ohman has some very nice yardage here. Do you have a pattern in mind?

MINNIE
I thought I'd use the one I have from Godey's Lady's Book; I've made it enough to feel comfortable cutting it.

LAVINIA
Oh, no, dear.  We can do better than that!  I'd guess it still has a bustle.

MINNIE
It does.

LAVINIA
The bustle died with the last century, thank goodness.  And without one,* you'll need ess fabric, so it's not as dear to spend a bit more on nicer yard goods.  I'll send over our hired girl with some new magazines and patterns. *(to forestall thanks)*  It's no trouble.

MINNIE
Well, I can't say I'll be sorry for the loss.  I never really understood them.

LAVINIA
This one is very pretty.  *(She holds up a length of fabric)* It would be very becoming with your hair color.  With black trim and buttons.

MINNIE
It's not too young?

LAVINIA
Not at all.

MINNIE
Arnie won't recognize me!

LAVINIA
He will so.  He'll be proud.

MR OHMAN
So this one, then?  How many yards?

MINNIE
Six? Seven? *(She looks down at herself)* I'll take what's left on the bolt; that's probably safest, goodness

knows I can't cut straight.  I also need some cornmeal- 5 pounds, and a half pound of tea.  Thank you, Mr. Ohman.

*HE moves away to collect these items.  LAVINIA looks through cards of buttons and notions.*

This was serendipitous, and I can't thank you enough.  I would have bought the gray.

LAVINIA
You're hardly old enough for that!  I'm glad I was here to save you from yourself.

MINNIE
You'll have to let me return the favor.

LAVINIA
Oh, my errand is terribly boring.  I'm nearly out of hair pins, and Mr. Williams broke the laces on his shoes.

MINNIE
How is Mr. Williams?

LAVINIA
He just returned from a business trip to Chicago and he's- in good health, thank you.  He's always in good health.

MINNIE
That's a comfort.

LAVINIA
Yes.  That is.

*The silence is about to get awkward when MR OHMAN returns with parcels.*

MR OHMAN
After subtracting your egg sales, the total was three dollars and twelve cents, Mrs. Erickson.

MINNIE
Well, my thirty cents didn't get me far!

MR OHMAN
You'll be pleased to know I took three cents off the poplin, in lieu of egg inflation.

MINNIE
*laughs.* That was very sporting of you. You'll put it on our bill?

MR OHMAN
Of course.

MINNIE
Can I see our account for a moment? Arnie says he stopped by last Friday, but he never remembers the total.

*He shows her the line in the account book.*

Hmmm. I see he restrained himself from buying yet another bridle. Thank you, Mr. Ohman. I'll be by on Saturday to settle it.

MR OHMAN
No trouble, Minnie. Can I assist you, Mrs. Williams?

LAVINIA
I need a pair of black shoelaces, this box of hairpins, and some boot black. Might as make the shoes worthy of the the new laces. *He collects the items as she talks.*

MR OHMAN
Twenty two cents.

LAVINIA
Yes, you can add it to our bill.

*MR OHMAN looks very uncomfortable.*

MR OHMAN
I can't.

LAVINIA
Why not?

MR OHMAN
You're welcome to take them now and send your hired girl over with the money later.

LAVINIA
But I can't add them to our account?

MR OHMAN *continues to look uncomfortable.*

MR OHMAN
Tomorrow would be fine, as well.

LAVINIA
*(incredibly embarrassed)* Is there a problem? I'm sure we can't be in arrears.

MR OHMAN
No, no. It's only that no purchases can be authorized by anyone other than the account holder.

LAVINIA
I don't understand. Minnie just charged her items, and surely her account is in her husband's name- oh.

MR OHMAN
It is at the discretion of the customer. I wo/uldn't

LAVINIA
/Yes. I understand, Mr. Ohman.

MINNIE
For twenty two cents, you can put it on mine.

LAVINIA
No! Thank you, no. *(pause)* Mr. Williams is very careful with accounts. He has a mania for accurate records.

MINNIE
I see.

LAVINIA
*(wearing frivolity like a shield)* He probably told me and I forgot; I'm very flighty that way. I can't remember anything from one day to another.

MINNIE
*(with complete understanding of her situation)* Neither can I. Not even my hat.

*LAVINIA does not cry.*

Not even pin money?

LAVINIA
No need! Everything is neatly anticipated. There is rarely a broken shoelace.

MINNIE
That's very...he is a banker, I suppose. That's why he's so wealthy, if you'll pardon me.

LAVINIA
He really might have told me that he had changed our terms of credit, and I don't remember. I'm often distracted.

MINNIE
Well, If Arnie had half his gumption when it came to finances/ we might be just as-

LAVINIA
/Minnie. No. Thank you. I'll send Anna over with the patterns.

*She leaves the purchases on the counter, and drifts away.*


Notes.

+*This is a real place, and the building still exists. Mr. E. F. Ohlman purchased it in 1902. Minnie and Lavinia, while not "real" people, have first names and last names taken from the 1900 census from Ogilivie. The Williams family was one of the most prominent in town, and the Ericksons were farmers.*

\**Godey's Lady's Book was an incredibly important source of fashion for rural women. They included a dress pattern in each issue, and copies of the magazine would be handed around families and communities. They stopped publication in 1898.*

**Since the Kids Are Gone...**

by Michael Long

*Michael Long is a playwright and freelance speechwriter. He also teaches writing at Georgetown University.*

**PRODUCTION HISTORY.** *Since the Kids Are Gone* had its world premiere September 7, 2012 by the Freshwater Theatre Company at the Nimbus Theatre in Minneapolis, Minnesota. A part of the Better (or) Worse festival, the production was directed by Nora Sachs, featuring Shannon Troy Jones and Elizabeth Olson.

*Professionals and amateurs are hereby warned that this material, being fully protected under the copyright laws of the United States and all other countries of the Copyright Union, is subject to royalty. All rights, including performance in any manner, are strictly reserved. No professional or nonprofessional performances of the play may be given without obtaining in advance the written permission of Michael Long. For production inquiries and other information, contact Michael Long directly at Mike@MikeLongOnline.com, or by phone at 703.408.7570.*

## LOCATION

The kitchen.

## CHARACTERS

Husband, 20s or older.

Wife, 20s or older.

## TIME

This morning.

*A man in a dark suit enters by the kitchen door, pretty much collapses at the dinette. Seconds later, his wife follows, dressed for a perfect spring day. She tosses her keys, rubs his neck. There's pleasure but no smiles.*

HUSBAND

Mmmm. That's good.

*She rubs a little more, offers a kiss. He pushes her away, gently.*

WIFE

You want to go upstairs?

*He shakes his head, no.*

WIFE

You sure?

*She kisses him again.*

WIFE (CONT'D)

Since the kids are gone --

*At this, he sits up.*

WIFE (CONT'D)

Well, they are.

*He pushes her away.*

HUSBAND

No.

WIFE

C'mon. Let's go upstairs.

HUSBAND

Is it okay if I don't feel like it?

WIFE

I never turn you down.

HUSBAND

I never ask when I know you don't want to.

WIFE

I never don't want to.

HUSBAND

I'm sorry you need it right now.

WIFE

So I'm the weird one?

HUSBAND

Spit out the gum.

WIFE

What do you care?

HUSBAND

Makes you look like a --

WIFE

What? Say it.

HUSBAND

Nothing.

WIFE

You're right, nothing.

*But... she spits her gum into a wrapper, pockets it.*

WIFE (CONT'D)

I'm going for cigarettes.

HUSBAND

Don't start smoking again.

WIFE

Can't go upstairs. Can't chew gum. Can't smoke.

HUSBAND

If we want to have another baby --

WIFE

I'm out of the baby business.

HUSBAND

I don't think that's just your decision.

WIFE

If you'd put out, we wouldn't be arguing.

HUSBAND

Is it okay if I don't feel like it?

WIFE

If you'd ever not felt like it.

*She pokes and prods him. No response.*

WIFE (CONT'D)

What is wrong with you?

*And then -- she freezes. The husband removes himself from her space, turns to the audience to address them.*

HUSBAND

This isn't normal for us. She wants to have sex, she doesn't have to beg. And if I want it, I sure don't have to beg. Which is exactly the problem. There was a time, my wife was... let's call it "uptight." Not terribly uptight. Modest, how about that? We tried a few things. And then, you know. Let's say she really came around. Because she did. Lucky me, right? Because I know there's not a lot of guys get a woman who'll do what she does. But you know? Sex has its place. Especially that kind of sex. And things have changed. I've changed.

*A beat, then he rejoins the scene.*

WIFE

You can do anything to me. What do you want?

*He ignores her.*

WIFE (CONT'D)

You know, all morning, I was thinking about, when the kids were born --

HUSBAND

I don't want to hear this --

WIFE

-- it was almost the end of the parties. Before, we could find some swinger ad, or we could drive down to the club and stay over. But when the kids came, we had to slow down. Remember the girl in the pink hat?

*He acknowledges it, barely.*

WIFE (CONT'D)

Remember how I asked her to come with us? And her husband just kissed her goodbye.

*She makes her way back to her husband and begins to touch him.*

WIFE (CONT'D)

I loved watching you with her. I was right up against her... right up against you... and do you remember what I did when she left?

*She kisses his neck. He's lost in it.*

WIFE (CONT'D)

Remember?

*He nods, yes, then freezes. Now she turns to address the audience.*

WIFE (CONT'D)

Since when do you offer a man sex and he turns it down? Especially him. We have a joke: If he's in an accident and the doctor says he's gone, I give him a blow job. He'll come back.

(a beat)

For the record? I used to be a prude -- well, that's strong. Let's say I was raised to be a nice girl. You save yourself for marriage, and after that, there are some things a nice girl doesn't do. But what do you get out of that, really? He wanted to try some things. I wanted to please him, and I was curious. I had no idea what I'd been missing. It was great. And then the kids came along... and it wasn't so great anymore. And now it's today, and we're alone, and he's like this.

*She suddenly rejoins the scene.*

WIFE (CONT'D)

Fuck me.

HUSBAND

Let's talk.

WIFE

You can talk while you're fucking me.

HUSBAND

Just sit down.

*She stares down at him. In a moment, he takes her hand. He finds some comfort in this, but she is barely able to tolerate him. Now he freezes. She withdraws, turns to the audience.*

WIFE (CONT'D)

Everybody's a little unsatisfied with how their life turns out, I get that. But that's different from having to drag yourself out of bed every morning because your whole miserable life is taking care of other people. I have a lot of catching up to do. And I know you're not supposed to say this, but I like my life better when the kids aren't here.

*She rejoins the scene.*

WIFE (CONT'D)

The sex doesn't have to mean anything.

HUSBAND

It always means something.

*She's shocked by this, really shocked.*

WIFE

Since when?

HUSBAND

You can't go rooting around in other people's pants like a box of cracker jacks and you're looking for a prize.

WIFE

Where did this come from?

HUSBAND

We've been living the wrong way.

WIFE

I've been living the wrong way?

HUSBAND

No, no. It's mostly my fault -- it *is* my fault.

WIFE

Like this -- today -- this is payback?

HUSBAND

How hard is that to believe?

WIFE

Now you're just wallowing in it.

HUSBAND

Well I'm entitled.

WIFE

Yeah?

*She was just responding, but now she's thinking. Yeah, he is entitled.*

WIFE (CONT'D)

Yeah. But I'm entitled, too. I want to feel better, and I need you to help me do that -- like you always do.

HUSBAND

So sex with me really doesn't mean anything.

WIFE

It's just sex, come on --

HUSBAND

You and I -- we have to change. We are through with the swinging and the parties and the other people. And I am finished treating you like a piece of meat.

*She freezes. He turns to the audience.*

HUSBAND (CONT'D)

It's so clear to me now. We all know, I just didn't want to believe it. Women get married because they want a whole life -- kids and stability and a man who takes care of them. Oh, it's not politically correct to say that, but that's what they want, you know it's true. And we were on track for that until I started this. I forced her to do these sick things because it was all about me. People say, how can you let your wife have sex with a stranger? Don't you respect her? But it wasn't about respect, it was about having fun. Some people play golf. We party. That's how far gone we were. And after this... it feels like sex ought to be more, like it's part of something bigger. Today I think about sex with some stranger, and it's like pissing all over something perfect. Do you know what I mean?

*He rejoins the scene.*

WIFE

I just want to empty out my head. Is that wrong? I need you to help me. Just like I help you. Remember when you got fired?

*He shoots her a look.*

WIFE (CONT'D)

Remember? We drove to Baltimore and spent the whole weekend in a hotel room answering crappy Craig's List ads so you could share me and forget how shitty you felt.

HUSBAND

I'm sorry.

WIFE

I don't want you to be sorry. I want you to remember.

*(a beat)*

You know the best time I ever had with you? The swinger's convention in Rehoboth Beach. Best time ever. Not even when Taylor was born --

HUSBAND

Don't say that --

WIFE

Not even after all those tests and doctor visits and Jean was born okay. Because those three days at the beach, all I had to do was feel good.

HUSBAND

We're not ever going back to Rehoboth.

WIFE

It's just sex. It didn't mean anything.

HUSBAND

It didn't mean anything with me?

WIFE

Oh, come on. If it meant anything, how could I do it with just anybody?

*She freezes. He addresses the audience.*

HUSBAND

There's the problem.

*(a beat)*

Sex is so consuming -- looking for it, anticipating it. Maybe the only way to keep that desire from wrecking everything else is to make it mean something. You find somebody special, and you make a promise about what you'll share with other people, and what you'll save just for her. And maybe the reward for doing that...

*He has an idea.*

HUSBAND (CONT'D)

-- maybe the reward is more than pleasure. Maybe it's a bond.

*A beat. He's putting it together....*

HUSBAND (CONT'D)

Maybe that's why people can stay with one person their whole lives. Maybe that's why some people don't kiss on the first date, I don't know. I just know I've missed out. I know what I have, and I know what I want. Tell ya this, I'm going to get our lives in order. This stuff? This is done. We're going to have a life. Head and heart. We're gonna make a promise. We're coming out of the gutter.

*He freezes. She addresses the audience.*

WIFE

You know what I've learned? I like feeling good, and sex is the top of the mountain. It's the most intense pleasure I've ever known, and there's not even the tiniest crack in that rock to slide in something else. Life is for pleasure. When he and I do what we do, it just takes me over, and I'm at the center of everyone's attention. My whole life -- first it was about what my parents wanted, and then it was about him --

*She gestures at her husband.*

WIFE (CONT'D)

-- and then it was all about the kids. Never about what I wanted. But the swinging? It's all about me. And that feels good. You know what? This is an opportunity. I'm not going to waste another minute of my life not feeling good.

*She returns to the scene.*

WIFE (CONT'D)

I want out of this marriage.

HUSBAND

*(laughing)*

Don't be dramatic.

WIFE

I wasn't sure. Now I'm sure.

HUSBAND

You're going to break up this marriage, today, because I won't have sex with you.

WIFE

Oh, come on. I don't want to be anybody's wife or anybody's mother --

HUSBAND

Well you don't have to worry about that anymore --

WIFE

Fuck you.

HUSBAND

I'm sorry, I'm sorry, I'm sorry, I didn't mean that, I'm so sorry --

*She steps away again.*

WIFE

You might have seen this on the news because it's just so.... We lost our children last week. Jean, Taylor. Both of them. School bus crash. They said it was quick, but how can you know? I would never wish that on anyone, but the fact is... I felt trapped here from the beginning, and the kids just made it worse. It's not that I didn't want them. It's just that I wanted me more. And when they died --

*A long moment.*

WIFE (CONT'D)

-- God forgive me, but it was like somebody threw open the door and said, here's your life back, here's a second chance. My parents were there and his parents and my brothers and sisters and all they could say was, oh, kids are the greatest joy, and you're young, you can have more kids... but the best times I remember are the times I was on my knees with some stranger in a motel in Rehoboth Beach, Maryland. I know how that sounds. But life is short. And here I am.

*A beat. For a moment, she is in both worlds.*

WIFE (CONT'D)

Well?

*And she returns to the scene.*

HUSBAND

You can't make a decision like that right now. The therapist said --

WIFE

The therapist --

*She trails off, laughing.*

HUSBAND

The therapist said we shouldn't make big decisions right now, not the day of the funeral.

WIFE

It's done.

HUSBAND

We can start over. I want us to be a family, not just with the kids. You and me. We have something. We can have something. I want to put all that other stuff behind us.

WIFE

I like all that other stuff.

HUSBAND

I thought you wanted this. I need you. I can get this right.

WIFE

The only thing we had right in the first place was the sex.

HUSBAND

Don't decide this today.

WIFE

It's done.

HUSBAND

No... no... no...

*A moment passes as a new reality sinks in. Now she administers a final test.*

WIFE

So... do you want to go upstairs? Since the kids are gone.

*They regard each other for a moment then, finally, she shakes her head, no. She turns to leave the house. She is almost gone when suddenly*

HUSBAND

Wait!

CURTAIN.

## SCARS

### By Greg Abbott

Greg Abbott is a playwright who lives in North Mankato, MN. His play is based on his wife's ordeal with breast cancer in 2011. During the past year, his short play "Vultures" was produced at the Minnesota Shorts Play Festival; "Amendments in my Pants" was produced by Box Wine Theatre in Minneapolis; "A Merry Frugal Christmas" was produced by Mankato Mosaic Theatre Company; and his full-length play, "Osama High" was given a reading at the Minneapolis Playwrights Center. He is a member of the Playwrights Project, based in Mankato, and also a member of the Minneapolis Playwrights Center and the Dramatist Guild. He is also known to steal all the best play ideas from his wife and son.

Contact:

Greg Abbott

805 Garfield Avenue

North Mankato, MN 56003

507-934-8133 (day)

507-345-1361 (evening)

gabbott@mnmsba.org

## SCARS

**Characters:**

MATT: Late 30-ish husband

KIT: A mid-30ish cancer survivor

**Setting:** Dining room in family's home

**Summary:** Kit is trying to cope with her fears about breast cancer and the fear that her husband, Matt, will be revolted by seeing her double mastectomy scar.

[KIT and MATT are in the dining room. KIT is wrapping up a box with mailing tape.]

MATT

Kit, come on. Is this even legal?

KIT

What? Of course it is. Not like I'm mailing anthrax or something.

MATT

You don't even know for sure that this is John Edwards' address.

KIT

I found it on Google.

MATT

Google?

KIT

Yeah.

MATT

I can't believe you're getting rid of them already. You only tried them once.

KIT

They're MY falsies. And I don't like them. I'm getting rid of them.

MATT

By mailing them to John Edwards.

KIT

Anyone who has an affair when his wife is in cancer recovery is an ass.

MATT

So what are you going to say when the postmaster asks if it is anything fragile, perishable or whatever? Gonna tell him it's your fake boobs?

KIT

I'm going to tell him it's fragile.

MATT

(considering) I guess it is. You gonna put a letter in there?

KIT

Already have it typed up.

[KIT pulls out the sheet of paper and reads it]

From one boob to another.

MATT (smiling)

Pretty funny. Glad I didn't leave you when you told me YOU had cancer.

[KIT stops wrapping and glances over at MATT]

KIT

Did you ever think of leaving me?

MATT

Come on! Leaving you just because you have cancer?

KIT

Leaving me because everything female about me is gone.

MATT

Kit, it is not. I didn't marry you for your boobs. I married YOU. I love YOU. You're going to beat this. You're a survivor. Breast cancer rates of recovery are… well, you know all about it. You checked out the entire breast cancer library at the Mayo. You know. We'll be fine.

KIT

Jessie hasn't asked me about it yet. She saw all the stitches and bandaging when I was changing. She pretended not to see it.

MATT

She's only ten. We talked to her. We told her we had to get the cancer out. She's fine with it. We'll talk to her again.

KIT

She's wondering if that's going to happen to her, too. She's wondering how freakish I'm going to look without any breasts.

MATT

You don't look freakish.

KIT

I do. I DO! You haven't seen my scar! I have. I had to look at my scar.

MATT

Well, you've never shown it to me. I know you're uncomfortable with me seeing it. But with your sister gone now, I'm going to have to help out. I've seen pictures of women with double mastectomies. It's OK. It will heal. It will be fine. Some women even tattoo flowers around it. They,

KIT

It's not just the scar, Matt. I'm talking about how I'm a woman with no breasts and pretty soon with no ovaries. I'm 35 and going into menopause. Think my mood swings are bad now? Just wait until my ovaries are yanked out. Then I get to deal with vaginal dryness, lack of sexual desire, hot flashes – just a shriveled up shell of an old woman. Then, see if you can stand it or if you pull a John Edwards.

MATT

I'm not going to pull a John Edwards.

    [MATT goes to hug her.]

KIT

Dammit, Matt. The doctors said you can't hug me. The scars have to heal. Don't want to break the stitch.

    [MATT backs away quickly]

MATT

Sorry. (pause) Sorry. I forgot.

    [KIT rips off another piece of tape for the box]

MATT
Kit. Come on. Don't be mad. I just forgot.

KIT

Don't know how you can forget. All these pads are like strapping sticks of dynamite around your chest.

MATT

Remember my strikes? We agreed I was bound to say or do something stupid during this. I get three strikes still, right?

KIT

It's down to one.

MATT

One? One? What else did I do?

KIT

What did you say when I called you from the doctor's office after he checked the lump? What did you say when I told you he found out it was invasive cancer?

MATT

Come on. It was a shock. We both thought it was just another swollen node. You've had false alarms before. The other two times.

KIT

To quote: (in low, manly mocking voice) "Ewww! That doesn't sound good."

MATT

OK, OK. That was before I read up on things. Before I…I know now. OK, I get the dumb schmuck award.

KIT

You didn't even offer to drive home from work to see me.

MATT

Alright. I've heard this way too many times. So…so mail me the other boob.

KIT

I only bought one set of falsies.

MATT

I know. Just kidding. See this smile? This is my just kidding face.

KIT

You ARE a boob.

MATT

That's me. See, having me around -- you won't ever miss your boobs.

KIT

(Pause) They're breasts, not boobs. (pause) Do you miss them?

MATT

Well, it's just…different. I mean, your breasts aren't what make you YOU. It doesn't matter if they're gone.

KIT

But you'll miss them. When, or if, we ever make love again, you'll miss them, won't you.

MATT

Well…no! I mean, well, kind of, but..

KIT

After the kissing, you always went right to my breasts.

MATT

Kit, yeah, but we'll do other things.

KIT

(sarcastically) Like fondle my scar? Suck on my scar?

MATT

No. Come on, Kit…

KIT

I feel like a fucking American Girl doll with no breasts and hollow on the inside. And I'm scared. I'm scared that after all this, the cancer will return and I won't get to see Jessie graduate. I'm scared that I've passed this on to Jessie, too. I'm scared that you won't find me attractive anymore. And I'm mad that there's so much fucking pressure to get implants. But I'm most afraid that this is turning me from a carefree young mother and wife into some bitter hag who'll drive you away. I'm like some androgynous mannequin at a store – you'd have better sex with an inflatable vagina.

[KIT starts to cry. MATT holds her hands.]

MATT

Kit. Remember: Let's stay positive. The doctor said it was important to stay positive. Keep a sense of humor. Cuz…cuz I've always been kind of scared of those androgynous mannequins and I'd probably never be able to blow up the inflatable vagina. Remember what I did to the camping tent air mattresses?

[KIT starts to laugh a little]

MATT

Yeah. Jammed that electronic air pump so far in that I couldn't get it out. Made my own Michelin Man. Like that Stay Puff Marshmallow Man in Ghostbusters.

KIT

And we never thought to just unplug it.

[KIT laughing a little more]

MATT

I'm an idiot. And you're stuck with me.

KIT

(Pause) You didn't answer my question.

MATT

I only have one strike left.

KIT

The strikes were just to keep you from being a total moron. There's always another inning after three strikes anyway, right? Honestly. I want you to answer honestly. I can get implants.

MATT

You don't want to get implants. It's a bunch of extra surgeries and you don't need them.

KIT

But maybe you need them. Maybe for the sake of our intimacy WE need them.

MATT

OK. Honestly, of course I'll miss them. But I had my time with them. We'll move on to other things. When I'm with you, I'm with you because you put up with me. I'm a bad kisser. Half the time I come early. I'm overweight. I mean, it's not like you have Johnny Depp in bed with you here.

KIT

That's for sure. (pause) So you don't mind if I skip the implants? I can wear falsies, but they seem unreliable. I read one woman went swimming and came out of the water with one sticking to the back of her leg. And when I tried to put them on, I couldn't. It was like seeing a cruel reminder of what I don't have.

MATT

I don't care if they fall down around your stomach. I don't care if you wear them at all. We talked this over. You don't need the extra surgeries. I'm fine without them. I'm fine with you the way you are.

KIT

You're fine with me all disfigured?

MATT

Kit, you're not disfigured. Just think of yourself as a pirate. Scars are cool. Johnny Depp has a scar. You love Johnny Depp. Pirates of the Caribbean?

KIT

His wife has breasts.

MATT

His wife doesn't have a cool scar.

KIT

If I showed my scar, you'd think again.

MATT

Kit, I've told you that you can show me the scar any time. In fact, your oncologist said you shouldn't be afraid to show the scar to me. It's not ugly. It's you as a survivor. It's you giving the finger to cancer. Besides, when you change the bandaging, I'm going to have to help. Your sister is gone. You're going to have to show me the scar. It's OK. I'm really fine with it.

KIT

You'll turn away. I can't even look at it without getting sick. The first time I changed the drain, I almost threw up. You might, too.

MATT

I went through the Mayo's sensitivity course for husbands, remember? They showed us pictures of women with mastectomies. I know what it looks like.

KIT

It's different in real life.

MATT

Well, I'm fine with it. You can show me any time. Show it to me now.

KIT

I'm not going to…not in the dining room.

MATT

Yeah. Right here. Right in the dining room. Jessie's at school. Nobody's here but me.

KIT

It's too bright. We need to turn out the lights.

MATT

If it's dark, how am I going to see the scar? It's almost a month now. It's time.

[KIT turns toward the package on the table]

KIT

I have to get this in the mail before noon. The postman…

MATT

I'll drop it off at the Post Office later.

KIT

Are you sure?

MATT

About the Post Office or seeing your scar?

KIT

The scar, stupid.

MATT

I'm sure. I want to see it. In fact, talking about all this -- you're turning me on.

KIT

Matt, this doesn't mean we're having sex. I'm not going to do it with a bunch of stitches and bandages across my chest.

MATT

We'll just try other things.

KIT

Other things? What other things?

MATT

Some English Grammar.

KIT

(confused) Grammar?

MATT

Yes, my English professor said I was quite the (emphasis slowly on each word) cunning linguist.

KIT

That is such a bad joke. You've ruined oral sex now, too.

MATT

Come on! It's funny.

KIT

It's old. And you're destroying the moment.

MATT

Right. Sorry.

KIT

Come here.

>[MATT walks over to her, and she holds his hands and looks into his eyes]

KIT

Before I do this, I just want you to know that I love you. And I know I'm not easy to…to get along with. And I don't want to be like this – like I'm in a big pity party. I know I'll beat this. I know I'll see Jessie's grandkids. I'm just in a little funk right now. I guess I've read way too much about husbands leaving their wives after a mastectomy. So thank you for staying with me. Thank you for not cheating on me or leaving me. Thank you for not…(starts to choke up)…not pressuring me to get the implants. Thank you for loving me…

>[KIT starts to cry as MATT kisses her]

MATT

Kit, I only wanted you. I want to get old with you. We'll see Jessie with her own family. Cancer – that scar – won't chase me away. Let me see it.

[KIT releases his hands and steps back, facing MATT with her back to the audience. She pulls down her shirt and steps out of it, exposing the camisole. Suddenly self-conscious, she turns away from him and faces the audience. MATT moves toward her, she puts one hand back to signal a stop.]

KIT

It's OK! (takes a deep breath – determined not to cry) I can do this.

[KIT turns back toward MATT, grabs her camisole and starts pulling apart the Velcro slowly. Lights out.]

## WAITING

### By Emily Arachtingi

e3tingi@yahoo.com

Emily Arachtingi served active duty in the US Army for four years. Though never deployed overseas, she was stationed on Fort Stewart, GA, during Operation Enduring Freedom and Operation Iraq Freedom. There she experienced firsthand the lives of the families of deployed soldiers. This memory of sacrifice and loss influenced *Waiting*, her first work ever performed onstage. Emily has worked as a stage manager for several theatre companies, including Freshwater Theatre, around the Twin Cities. She plans on continuing writing about this subject and more, and hopefully having more pieces produced in the future.

I understand, Becky; it's been seven months and part of me wishes I had gone home, too. Waiting here is so hard. My parents say the weather at home is lovely: all the gardens are in bloom and the planting's begun, but the mosquitos haven't come out yet. And here the temperature's been in the nineties with humidity the same for the past two weeks.

I did move back, the second deployment. I took the kids back to my parents' house in Inver Grove Heights. Having the grandparents around was wonderful, I'll admit. Overall, Minnesota was nice enough, but it was difficult to try to adjust to living surrounded by civilians and so far away from the unit wives. They're a support group that just doesn't exist there. I can talk about it to my coworkers and my nonmilitary friends, but they can't understand. I had one try to tell me that her husband being sent away for a conference for two weeks was similar to Jake being gone for seven months in a place where a good portion of the populace wants to kill him just for being there. Others just try to be sympathetic, but they don't get it. So when Jake was deployed for a third and fourth time, I just stayed on base, waiting in a familiar environment.

Jamie and Elijah, the boys, are now old enough that school becomes an issue as well. I want them to have what stability they can, growing up as normally as possible, for military brats. When Jake gets back from deployment, we're due to PCS, which is being assigned to a new duty station, but the orders aren't due to come for another month or two. So that means another new school, another new set of friends to make, for both them and me. At least here with the three-twenty-fifth everyone's been friendly and accepting, a good group of mothers and wives and one husband (though maybe not legally yet). Even Sarah, Lieutenant Chase's wife, is okay, not too stuck up to hang with the noncom's wives. Not every unit you'll encounter is like that. I'll miss everybody when we PCS.

The weekly get-togethers of unit families for dinner make for a pretty nice routine. I'm always in charge of the bread, since I'm the only one who bakes bread. Brian grows his own vegetables, so in a month we'll be enjoying the fresh squash and beans and tomatoes that make the kids (and a few of the younger wives) roll their eyes and huff. This week Sarah's doing a lasagna bake, which is a heck of a lot better than Tamara, PFC McCullough's wife, the redhead with the pizza last week. Must admit, though, pizza was well received by the kids. Between that and the pop, they were ecstatic to have a dinner of junk food. I'd feel better about it if we didn't eat out so much, but I'm so busy trying to work and keep up with their schedules that some days it's not an option to fix a normal meal. We're single parents during these deployments.

I think it's important that we meet like this, especially this week. No one's heard from their husbands in two weeks. We all kinda knew that this was part of the deal, being a military wife, but it's hard for you and the other young wives who haven't been through a deployment yet. Jake and I have been through this deployment and return three times already, though I'll admit it never gets easier. At least it's not as bad as during the start of Operation Iraqi Freedom, when everyone was stop-lossed, which means the deployments kept being extended. The waiting never gets easier.

Jake's first OIF deployment was terrifying. I stayed at Fort Lewis for that. He was extended for five months, possibly the worst five months of my life. Reports kept coming in with crisp young captains and lieutenants in their blues going from house to house, beautifully dressed grim reapers. Those left behind clung together and prayed that those visits were not for us. Seven times our little group of spouses met those men and helped the poor widow put her affairs in order and go back to whatever family she had left. We still live in fear of those messengers of death, even now when the reports are infrequent.

Jamie was only a year old at the time and was almost two by the end of that deployment. When Jake returned home, Jamie didn't know his father. If Elijah hadn't been so excited to see daddy, I think Jamie might have been terrified and not even smiled at Jake. He's always been the more timid of the boys. Thank heavens Elijah is such a good boy, always looking out for his little brother, even though he's seven years older.

So this is the fourth deployment for our family. I feel like an old hand at it, able to guide you newer wives -and husband- through your first time. Tonight the boys stayed at home to play video games, the same as their father plays off-duty in Kandahar. Jake always tells them on Skype that when he gets back they better be able to beat him, so I can't really get mad at them for playing as long as their homework and chores are done. It's probably good they aren't here. Two weeks. That's a pretty long time, especially for what Jake described as a routine patrol into some valley not too far from the base. Don't worry too much, though. There haven't been any stories on the news, so there's nothing definitely wrong. Nothing to do at this point except wait. I hate waiting.

Now who could that be? Everyone who said they would come is here. Maybe one of the others changed their plans?

Oh god, that's an officer pulling up to the house. In his blues. Becky, get Sarah now please. Oh, wait, she's already at the door, like a good platoon leader. All right, you get the other adults. Quietly please, it's most likely nothing but we don't want to start worrying the kids.

Everyone here? Good. It's probably nothing, there's been no reports of action in the news for the past two weeks. You could hear a pin drop in this room. Don't worry, honey. We're together, everything will be okay.

Here comes Sarah now, followed by that captain. Her face, I've never seen her so pale. Sarah? What is it? An IED on the way back to Kandahar hit one of the vehicles and ...

Becky, Becky, please, stand up. Honey, it'll be okay. I've got you, sweetie.

Sarah? Why are you sorry?

What do you mean... Oh my god, no. Jake, too?

Freshwater Theatre Press

**A SMALL PLAY ABOUT MARRIAGE**
By Jen Scott
octoberdandy@gmail.com
612-387-1020cell
www.octoberdandy.com

Jen Scott is a Twin Cities-based theater artist. Recent performance credits include work with Walking Shadow Theater Company, Red Eye Theater, HUGE Theater, Hennepin Theater Trust and others. She teaches at the Brave New Workshop, Park Square Theater, Children's Theater Company; writing credits include pieces for the Science Museum of Minnesota and Chicago Avenue Project. Details and general shenanigans can be found at octoberdandy.com.

## Characters
WOMAN (could possibly be triple cast as Jane and Cherry)
Herb, white 30something, newly married
Ali, white 30something, newly married
Hank, white, in a relationship with Adam
Adam, african-american, in a relationship with Hank
Cherry, newly wed
Jane, 30something, in a relationship with a woman

*Black stage.*

*Woman appears (possibly with a flashlight under her face, ala campfire storytelling).*

### WOMAN
Once upon a time, there was a funny place called the world. And the world created things - - and gave them life and, because everything needs an ending, also gave them death. Bacteria and plants and fish. Legs and skin and teeth. The bacteria created sex, and everyone thought it was a fine idea. The animals created affection and dislike, love and hate and fear.

The Humans thought a lot. They were very clever. And they borrowed wonderful things from the animals, like tools and laughter. And they created amazing things, like toilets and lightbulbs. They created so many things, that they needed to invent invisible things, just to control what had been made. And they got so used to controlling objects, that some felt that it might be easier if they could just control each other.

And has people tend to do, a woman and man and a woman and a woman and a man and a man fell in love.

That should be enough.

But sometimes, they loved each other enough that they'd want to stay together until their end. And this was such an important thing, that they wanted to shout it to the heavens. Or at least have a party.

*Yard chairs in a circle. Late night party backyard sort of thing. Some beer cans and dirty paper plates by the chairs. Maybe some cheap paper wedding decorations. A couple, Hank and Adam, are talking.*

### Hank
It's fear-bating! That's what it is! Hateful fear-bating. Never underestimate the white man's potential for evil.

### Adam

Hank - - you're a white man. You're the person in power. Besides - - are we're really doing this? Technically, this is a wedding reception. For someone else. Besides - -

**Hank**
Nooooo - - I can't marry. I can destroy nations, but I can't marry. I'm like Godzilla!

**Adam**
Really.

**Hank**
I'm one of them! I came out this way! I'm fucking Godzilla and I didn't even ask to be. Was it any wonder I was so mopey as a teenager… "Doesn't anyone see how much pain I'm in? I'm gay and I can't tell anyone!!!" I had no clue. I couldn't step out of my own shoes for one second. "Black people have got it so great - - they're so cool and their struggle is so public."

**Adam**
God, you're an idiot. I love you. But you're an idiot.

**Hank**
All of my struggle was so secret. There was no way to out myself - - unless I did something active. No passive outing. And I was too scared.

**Adam**
That's common. Hank - - You were a TEENAGER.

**Hank**
So?

**Adam**
Everyone's stupid as a teenager. Everyone's all about their friends or their cock. Everyone's neurotic. Some of us still are. You're okay.

**Hank**
I don't know what else I can do. I don't like feeling powerless. I've made myself feel powerless for so long, and now someone else STILL gets to decide what rights I'm privy to.

**Adam**
Stop talking that way. Things change. Plus, no one stopped you from marrying me…

**Hank**
It's not official.

**Adam**
To me, it is. To Iowa, it might be.

**Hank**

As gay Godzilla, I should be able to officially marry whoever the hell I want.

**Adam**
Gaydzilla?

**Hank**
You're making fun of me.

**Adam**
No. I'm telling you that you're drunk. And that you need to step back. We have a good life. We have good friends. And things sometimes feel out of our control. But things will change.

**Hank**
I want to officially officially marry you. Not in a commitment ceremony sort of way. Commitment ceremonies are so very 90s.

**Adam**
I thought our's was fine.

**Hank**
Really - - How can this not work you up? How are you not mad? How are you less drunk than me?

**Adam**
Because I don't drink shitty beer and I'm not from Wisconsin.

*Black out on the campfire.*

*Herb & Ali enter, chatting...*

**Herb**
I've never met them?

**Ali**
They were at our wedding.

**Herb**
I don't remember them.

**Ali**
It think they might have been in the bathroom.

**Herb**
Wait.. were they the ones smoking up in the bathroom?

**Ali**
.. probably. I know they didn't stay very long.

**Herb**
Will they be smoking tonight?

**Ali**
They probably already have.

**Herb**
This is their wedding reception!

**Ali**
And it's also a picnic potluck barbeque. And it's their's. They can be high if they want to.

**Herb**
I hate the smell of pot.

**Ali**
I know. I'm sorry.

**Herb**
The smell makes me nauseous. I totally have flashbacks.

**Ali**
Shush.

**Herb**
I get the marijuana shudders. I have pot PTSD.

**Ali**
I don't think that's even possible.

*Door immediately opens. Cherry appears, wearing a veil and a fun dress.*

**Cherry**
HIIII!!!! Ali, you look amazing! Is this Herbert? Herbert, it's so awesome to see you again! Thank you for coming!

**Herb**
Just Herb is fine.

**Cherry**
Speaking of.. we have, and we're sharing.. so if you'd like..

**Herb**
I'm good. Serious.

**Ali**

We brought homemade beer.

**Cherry**
That's amazing. Everyone's outback, make yourself at home. Food's everywhere. Most of my family's left. The fire's started. There's dead things.

**Herb**
We brought some veggie burgers too.

**Ali**
Herb's a veggie.

**Cherry**
That's great. The grill is currently looks like a slaughterhouse, but we can find some room.

**Herb**
*Holds up beer* Fridge?

**Cherry:**
There's a cooler out back. Be brave.

*Herb exits.*

**Ali**
Congratulations!!!!!!

**Cherry**
Thank you so much for coming!

**Ali**
How was the ceremony?

**Cherry**
Short. This is so much better. All I wanted was a cook out. This dress smells like charcoal and I almost set the veil on fire. It's so good to see you! How's married life?

**Ali**
Great. Happy. Really happy.

**Cherry**
That's so great. Make yourselves at home! You know your way around.

*Cherry dances away just as Herb re-enters.*

**Herb**
Wow.

**Ali**
That's Cherry. She's awesome.

**Herb**
She's intense.

**Ali**
She gets really excited when she smokes up. Or.. you know. Gets married.

**Herb**
This is the weirdest wedding reception I've ever been to.

**Ali**
It's not *that* weird. Glass houses, Herb. We had your brother in a stormtrooper uniform.

**Herb**
That was maybe a little weird.

**Ali**
THIS. Right now. *This* is weird.

**Herb**
What is?

**Ali**
You. Here. In this house.

**Herb**
It looks like every other house in Minneapolis.

**Ali**
I've spent so much time in this house.

**Herb**
Pre- me?

**Ali**
Pre- you.

**Herb**
Things change.

**Ali**
I don't recognize my life anymore

**Herb**

What?

**Ali**
I don't recognize my life anymore. I used to me Ali who lived in Northeast with a garden and drug dealing neighbors and maybe one day I would own chickens. I'm not that anymore.

**Herb**
But you are.

**Ali**
I'm not. I live in an apartment in Uptown. I buy groceries at an overpriced boutique. I'm.. happy.

**Herb**
But who you were, and are, is who I married.

**Ali**
No. You married who I am *with* you. ... Don't you feel any different? Why is this... us... so easy for you? Not being Herb, but being Herb and Ali. I'm not saying it's NOT easy for me. I'm happy. But... you know.

**Herb**
...It feels different, but.. it feels natural. It feels like a natural extension of who I've become. I've changed so much over the last ten years. It's only now that I was ready for you.

**Ali**
Or anybody else.

**Herb**
Not anybody else.

**Ali**
Or *someone* else.

**Herb**
.. yeah. I guess. Or someone else.

**Ali**
I don't want a divorce.

**Herb**
What? Neither do I!

**Ali**
Ever. No divorce ever. I hate the idea of losing what we've started.

**Herb**

We're not getting a divorce.

**Ali**
But even if we did, we'd just find someone else. And make it work.

**Herb**
What? Ali, we just got married.

**Ali**
I don't know what we'll be in five years.

**Herb**
We're not supposed to know.

**Ali**
What if I change?

**Herb**
I hope you do.

**Ali**
What?

**Herb**
Not in that way! .. The point is, we've agreed to stand next to each other - - no matter what. And we're both going to change. That's the deal, the agreement, we made. It's a good deal.

**Ali**
A marriage isn't an agreement.... It's a plan. It's a plan that constantly changes. It's a choose your own adventure book, but the outcome is always that you stay together. Until you don't.

**Herb**
And that's okay?

**Ali**
It's what's important to me. It's what I want.

**Herb**
… So you didn't marry me for the tax deduction?

**Ali**
Maybe a little bit. And half of your doll collection.

**Herb**
They're not dolls. They're action figures.

### Ali
I love you.

### Herb
I love you too.

### Ali
But even just the fact we're saying that to each other. The fact that we ended up together. Isn't it just.. weird?

*Lights down on Herb & Ali. Lights up on a single woman with a beer can, possibly in the kitchen..*

### Jane
We've been trying to get pregnant for almost two years now. .. It's hard. It's fine. We wanted to do a 'womb' trade.. I'd have the first baby, Marie would have the second. ...We don't know why it doesn't work. It could be anything. We flew to Tulum last December, the descent into Cancun was super steep. We had sex while I was pregnant, that's not supposed to harm anything, but you don't know. Maybe I ate some wheat.

It's strange. It's strange that Marie's mom didn't like me at first, didn't like the idea of her princess being with a girl - - she'd visit, and I'd be on pins and needles. And now that we're trying to have a baby, it's sweetness and light. She buys me things at garage sales. She actually asked to talk with me over the phone. I never know what to say.

I want to grow old with Marie. I want to make a family. I want to ride in the ambulance with her, and not follow behind in a car, sobbing. I just want to be us.

*Lights slowly up on the entire stage. All are present in their separate spaces, or maybe facing the audience.*

### Ali
You are the person who knows me best, but you're so new to me. And YOU'LL KEEP CHANGING.

### Hank
I find it hard to believe that most people are interested in what we do in the bedroom. And who we do it with. Why do they care?

### Jane
I think it's ridiculous that Marie and I being together only becomes relevant if we're not just two women living some "morally ambiguous" lifestyle together. But instead, we're weirdly accepted if we have some greater purpose. If we're MOTHERS.

We are together because we're together. We'll have children to add and share in that love that's already there! We're together because we love each other.

### Herb
I'm not perfect. I'll never be perfect. For better or worse, I'll keep changing. And, I promise, I'll never

leave.

**Adam**
They care because they can make you feel less. Make you feel worse. They want to make sure that you know that what you're doing is weird and not right. They want to make you feel more than you should. And what we need to remember, is that, what we have, it's not their's to say no to. It's not their's to control.

**Ali**
Married people leave all the time!

**Hank**
How's married life?

**Jane**
How's married life?

**Adam**
How's married life?

**Herb**
How's married life?

**Ali**
How's married life?

*Stage lights down slowly, back to WOMAN, flashlight under her face again?*

**WOMAN**
And the people fell in love and out of love. And some people, looking for power, scared of what was to be, tried to control and define.

This funny place, the world, doesn't work that way. It never has, and never will. No matter how many invisible things attempt to confine what is or what will be, control is just a story that scared people tell each other.

Change is good. Change leads to knowledge, knowledge kills fear and ignorance. And so the humans moved forward the best way they could. With parties. And celebrations. And hope. And with love.

**The Entr'actes**
Curated and Directed by Scot Moore
scotmoore@gmail.com

Scot Moore graduated from UW-River Falls with a degree in Theatre and Broadcast Journalism and has worked in theatre as an actor, director, producer, and designer for 15 years. He's also a playwright and musician and is very happy to lend his many hats to Freshwater Theatre. As an actor, he's worked with Starting Gate, Theatre in the Round, Bedlam Theatre, Nimbus Theatre, Epic Arts Repertory Theatre, Commedia Beauregard, Cromulent Shakespeare Co, Way to Go Turbo, and more.

Scot has mostly dedicated his theatrical free time to the production end of Freshwater Theatre while undergoing a lengthy process of minor facial reconstruction (it's a long story). Scot recently made his professional directing debut here in the Twin Cities with Freshwater's recent production of The Book of Liz, September 2011 at Nimbus Theater in Minneapolis. Scot is returned to the stage after this hiatus to play Dan in Going Down on the Queen of Minneapolis, and also designed sound for Better (or) Worse. For more about Scot, and for samples of his writing, please visit: www.scotmoore.net

His novel, *Gaymerica*, is available for purchase locally and on Amazon.com.

"Better or Worse" was not a project designed to make commentary one way or another about religion. However, it is impossible to look at gender rights issues and not see how religion is used as a wedge to divide our culture. As such, it seemed appropriate to offer a selection of marriage-related material from various religious texts. In doing so, we found varied and complex thoughts from five major religions - some of which did not address marriage directly at all, but rather depth of relationships between individuals.

These are the passages used to sample those marriage beliefs and thoughts:

Hindu Material:
- Sītārāma Sahagala. "Hindu Marriage and Its Immortal Traditions." Navyug Publications, 1969.

Jewish Material
- Deuteronomy 22: 13-21
- Ruth 1: 16-17

Muslim Material
- The Qur'an, Book 2: 223-228
- The Qur'an, Book 4: 3-4

Christian Material
- Ephesians 5: 28-33
- Hebrews 13: 1-6

Buddhist Material
- Laurie Sue Brockway. "Your Interfaith Wedding." Praeger, 201